Machine Learning with Python:
A Practical Beginners' Guide

Book 2 in the Machine Learning for Beginner's series

Oliver Theobald

Published by Scatterplot Press

First Edition

Copyright © 2019 by Oliver Theobald

Published by Scatterplot Press

All rights reserved. No part of this publication may be reproduced, distributed, or transmitted in any form or by any means, including photocopying, recording, or other electronic or mechanical methods, without the prior written permission of the publisher, except in the case of brief quotations embodied in critical reviews and certain other non-commercial uses permitted by copyright law.

www.scatterplotpress.com

ISBN: 9781686658495

Please contact the author at **oliver.theobald@scatterplotpress.com** for feedback, media contact, omissions or errors regarding this book.

FIND US ON:

Newsletter

http://eepurl.com/gKjQij

Enjoy book recommendations, free giveaways of future book releases from the author, and other blog posts and news concerning machine learning, trends, and data science.

Teachable

www.scatterplotpress.com

For introductory video courses on machine learning.

Skillshare

www.skillshare.com/user/machinelearning_beginners

For introductory video courses on machine learning and video lessons from other instructors.

Instagram

machinelearning_beginners

For mini-lessons, book quotes, and more!

TABLE OF CONTENTS

FOREWORD 5

DATASETS USED IN THIS BOOK 10

INTRODUCTION 12

DEVELOPMENT ENVIRONMENT 21

MACHINE LEARNING LIBRARIES 25

EXPLORATORY DATA ANALYSIS 32

DATA SCRUBBING 46

PRE-MODEL ALGORITHMS 61

SPLIT VALIDATION 82

MODEL DESIGN 88

LINEAR REGRESSION 100

LOGISTIC REGRESSION 117

SUPPORT VECTOR MACHINES 133

κ-NEAREST NEIGHBORS 144

TREE-BASED METHODS 154

NEXT STEPS 174

APPENDIX 1: INTRO TO PYTHON 175

APPENDIX 2: PRINT COLUMNS 183

FOREWORD

While it's luring to see trends rise quickly, it's important to see long periods of resilience before the curve. For those pursuing a career in machine learning, it's reassuring to know this field of study not only predates the Internet and the moon landing but also most readers of this book.

Machine learning is not an overnight movement and the path to the present day has been anything but smooth sailing. Conceptual theories emerged in the 1950s but progress was stalled by computational constraints and limited data. This resulted in a logjam of research and good intentions as theoretical models of prediction, algorithm design, and extrapolation of future possibilities accumulated in research institutions until powerful processing chips and large datasets emerged in the 1990s. Renewed interest helped to breach the gap between theory and capability during this decade but it still wasn't enough to push field-altering breakthroughs in the space of deep learning.

That breakthrough came in 2009 when Adjunct Professor Andrew Ng and his team at Stanford University experimented with tethering gaming chips—better known for image rendering—to solve complex data problems. The combination of inexpensive GPU (graphic processing unit) chips and compute-intensive algorithms pushed the lead domino in the development of deep learning. This crucial breakthrough coalesced with other developments in reinforcement learning to spark a surge in interest, an oversupply of newspaper analogies to Hollywood movies, and an international hunt for AI talent.

In 2016, media interest climbed to a new high at the glitzy Four Seasons Hotel in Seoul, where TV cameras locked lenses on an 18-by-18 Go board with the world champion on one side and an AI program on the other. The game of Go consists of billions of permutations and commentators described the then world champion, Lee Sodol, as having a sixth sense for interpreting the state of play. His opponent was AlphaGo, a sophisticated deep learning model designed to outperform any opponent—mortal or synthetic.

The team of human developers responsible for designing the AlphaGo program scarcely knew the rules of the game when they began work on the project, but they watched on excitedly as AlphaGo performed its first move.

The AI model unsettled Lee early—forcing him to take a nervous cigarette break—before systemically defeating the South Korean four games to one. News headlines of AlphaGo's cold and mechanistic victory beamed across the globe—as had been the case with other televised AI feats before it. Predictably, these reports focused on the superiority of machine intelligence over humans.

Contrary to these initial headlines, the 2017 Netflix documentary *AlphaGo* helped to later realign attention towards the human ingenuity behind AlphaGo's victory. The documentary details the lead-up to Seoul and in doing so shines the light on a team of talented employees thriving in a new and far-reaching line of work.

Dressed in casual attire, the AlphaGo team can be seen working hard behind their screens stocking the model with training data, optimizing its hyperparameters, and coordinating vital computational resources before extracting game tactics from human experts honed over many years of competition.

Despite its prolific success, the AlphaGo program has not replaced any of the programmers that worked on its source code or taken away their salaries. In fact, the development of AlphaGo has helped to expand the size and profile of the company DeepMind Technologies, which was acquired by Alphabet Inc earlier in 2014.

Working in AI

After two AI winters and ongoing battles for academic funding, we have entered a golden age in industry employment. Complex databases, fast and affordable processing units, and advanced algorithms have rejuvenated established fields of human expertise in mathematics, statistics, computer programming, graphics, and visualization as well as good old problem-solving skills.

In a global job market steadily automated and simplified by Web 2.0 technology, the field of machine learning provides a professional nirvana for human ingenuity and meaningful work. It's a cognitively demanding occupation; one that goes far beyond tuning ad campaigns or tracking web traffic on side-by-side monitors. With jobs in this industry demanding expertise in three distinct fields, achieving machine intelligence is far from easy and demands a high level of expertise.

The ideal skillset for a machine learning developer spans coding, data management, and knowledge of statistics and mathematics. Optional areas of expertise include data visualization, big data management, and practical experience in distributed computing architecture. This book converges on the vital coding part of machine learning using Python.

Released in 1991 by Guido van Rossum, Python is widely used in the field of machine learning and is easy to learn courtesy of van Rossum's emphasis on code readability. Python is versatile too; while other popular languages like R offer advantages in advanced mathematical operations and statistical functions, they offer limited practical use outside of hard data crunching. The utility of Python, however, extends to data collection (web scraping) and data piping (Hadoop and Spark), which are important for sending data to the operating table. In addition, Python is convertible to C and C++, enabling practitioners to run code on graphic processing units reserved for advanced computation.

The other advantages of learning a popular programming language (such as Python) are the depth of jobs and the spread of relevant support. Access to documentation, tutorials, and assistance from a helpful community to troubleshoot code problems cannot be overlooked and especially for anyone beginning their journey in the complex world of computer programming.

As a practical introduction to coding machine learning models, this book falls short of a complete introduction to programming with Python. Instead, general nuances are explained to enlighten beginners without stalling the progress of experienced programmers. For those new to Python, a basic overview of Python can be found in the Appendix section of this book. It's also recommended that you spend 2-3 hours watching introductory Python tutorials on YouTube or Udemy if this is your first time working with Python.

What You Will Learn

As the second book in the *Machine Learning for Beginner's Series,* the key premise of this title is to teach you how to code basic machine learning models. The content is designed for beginners with general knowledge of machine learning, including common algorithms such as logistic regression and decision trees. If this doesn't describe your experience or you're in need of a refresher, I have summarized key concepts from machine learning in the opening chapter and there are overviews of specific algorithms dispersed throughout the book. For a gentle and more detailed explanation of machine learning theory minus the code, I suggest reading the first title in this series *Machine Learning for Absolute Beginners (Third Edition)*, which is written for a more general audience.

Finally, it's important to note that as new versions of Python code libraries become available, it's possible for small discrepancies to materialize between the code shown in this book and the actual output of Python in your development environment. To clarify any discrepancies or to help troubleshoot your code, please contact me at oliver.theobald@scatterplotpress.com for assistance. General code problems can also be solved by searching for answers on Stack Overflow (www.stackoverflow.com) or by Google searching the error message outputted by the Python interpreter.

Conventions Used in This Book
- *Italic* indicates the introduction of new technical terms
- `lowercase bold` indicates programming code in Python
- the terms "target variable" and "output" are used interchangeably
- the terms "variable" and "feature" are used interchangeably
- Typical of machine learning literature, "independent variables" are expressed as an uppercase "X" and the "dependent variable" as a lowercase "y"

DATASETS USED IN THIS BOOK

For issues accessing and downloading these datasets, please contact the author at oliver.theobald@scatterplotpress.com

Advertising Dataset

Overview: This dataset contains fabricated information about the features of users responding to online advertisements, including their sex, age, location, daily time spent online, and whether they clicked on the target advertisement. The dataset was created by Udemy course instructor Jose Portilla of Pierian Data and is used in his course *Python for Data Science and Machine Learning Bootcamp*.

Features: 10

Missing values: No

File name: `advertising.csv`

Link: http://scatterplotpress.com/p/datasets

Melbourne Housing Market Dataset

Overview: This dataset contains data on house, unit, and townhouse prices in Melbourne, Australia. This dataset comprises data scraped from publicly available real estate listings posted weekly on www.domain.com.au. The full dataset contains 21 variables including address, suburb, land size, number of rooms, price, longitude, latitude, postcode, etc.

Features: 21

Contains missing values: Yes

File name: `Melbourne_housing_FULL.csv`

Link: https://www.kaggle.com/anthonypino/melbourne-housing-market/#Melbourne_housing_FULL.csv

Berlin Airbnb Dataset

Overview: Airbnb has exploded in growth following its humble beginnings in 2008, and Berlin is one of the biggest markets for alternative accommodation in Europe, with over 22,552 Airbnb listings recorded as of November 2018. The dataset contains detailed data, including location, price, and reviews, and was created by Murray Cox.

Features: 16

Contains missing values: Yes

File name: `listings.csv`

Link: http://scatterplotpress.com/p/datasets

Kickstarter Dataset

Overview: Kickstarter.com is the world's largest crowd-funding platform for creative projects and this dataset was created using data extracted from the Kickstarter website.

Features: 35

Contains missing values: Yes

File name: `18k_Projects.csv`

Link: https://www.kaggle.com/tayoaki/kickstarter-dataset

INTRODUCTION

As an empirical and specialized field of data science and a dominant sub-field of AI, machine learning[1] describes the ability of computer models to learn from data and perform cognitive reasoning without direct programming.[2] This is a process known as *self-learning*—an exciting but somewhat vague concept that underpins machine learning. While the human programmer maintains ownership of variable selection and setting algorithm learning hyperparameters (settings), the decision model interprets patterns and generates an output without a direct command. This course of action serves as a major distinction from traditional computer programming where computers are designed to produce fixed outputs in response to pre-programmed commands.

The initial blueprints for machine learning were conceived by Arthur Samuel while working for IBM as an engineer in the late 1950s. Samuel defined machine learning as a subfield of computer science that provides computers the ability to learn without being explicitly programmed.[3] Incorporating probability theory and statistical modeling, Samuel outlined the potential for machines to detect patterns and improve performance based on

---

[1] The word "machine" was a common byname for computers during this time and the moniker has stuck over the decades.
[2] Aurélien Géron, "Hands-On Machine Learning with Scikit-Learn and TensorFlow: Concepts, Tools, and Techniques to Build Intelligent Systems," *O'Reilly Media*, 2017.
[3] Arthur Samuel, "Some Studies in Machine Learning Using the Game of Checkers," *IBM Journal of Research and Development*, Vol. 3, Issue. 3, 1959.

data and empirical information; all without direct programming commands.

Samuel held that by using data as input, machines could mimic the ability of humans to learn and identify optimal decisions without explicit code commands from the programmer. While human programmers were required to facilitate the input of data and the selection of algorithm(s), they would forego the role of rule-maker under Samuel's radical new theory.

In 1959, Samuel published a paper in the *IBM Journal of Research and Development* investigating the application of machine learning in the game of checkers. The goal of his research was to program a computer to gradually exceed the capabilities of the person who programmed it. The machine was designed to assess the state of a checkers board and incorporated probability theory to identify a move that would best lead to a winning outcome. After each game, the program integrated experience and logged new strategies to refine its performance for play against the next opponent. This process repeated until the computer program was able to consistently beat its programmer.

Samuel's chess program held a competitive edge over symbolic systems that were in vogue at this time and which relied on pre-programmed knowledge. Unlike symbolic systems, human experts weren't needed to predefine steps or game strategy. Instead, the machine developed intelligence by reviewing data to determine patterns and then codifying these patterns to inform game strategy. Validation of Samuel's work came in 1961 when his checkers program claimed victory in a live match played against a professional and competitively ranked human player.

While Samuel made significant progress in machine learning research and model design during his time at IBM, it wasn't until after his retirement in 1966 that the full scope of his findings spread to the broader artificial intelligence community. According to the authors of *Human + Machine: Reimagining Work in the Age of AI*, Paul R. Daugherty and H. James Wilson, news of

Samuel's work was partly inhibited by his modest character and reluctance to self-promote.[4]

Over the next two decades, attention took a backseat as other fields of artificial intelligence including symbolic systems and expert systems[5] took precedence in industry and academic funding. Artificial intelligence, itself, underwent two periods of declined interest, better known as the two AI winters.

The dot-com era in the 1990s eventually revived investment in machine learning as a solution to maximize the value of data collected from online retail and digital systems. While it seems trivial now, access to a large and cheap supply of data to facilitate learning was a major constraint for AI researchers before this period. Drastic advances in computer storage and processing capacity also provided the infrastructure desperately needed to cross the chasm between theory and practical application.

A new supply of data and cheap computing power handed machine learning a decisive victory over expert systems as it became more efficient to derive knowledge from data rather than task experts to configure code as an elaborate series of if/else rules. Machine learning also offered a comparative advantage in tackling complex and unknown problems where known steps of reasoning and action weren't available, such as detecting fraud and classifying spam email messages.

Dependent and Independent Variables

As with other fields of statistical inquiry, machine learning is based on the cross-analysis of dependent and independent variables. The dependent variable (y) is the output you wish to predict and the independent variable (X) is an input that supposedly impacts the dependent variable (output). The goal of

---

[4] Paul R. Daugherty and H. James Wilson, "Human + Machine: Reimagining Work in the Age of AI," *Harvard Business Review Press*, 2018.
[5] Systems that enabled machines to perform rudimentary reasoning using if/else rules as an alternative to strict predetermined code.

machine learning is to then find how the independent variable/s (X) affect the dependent variable (y).

To predict the value of a house, for example, a machine learning framework called supervised learning analyzes the relationship between house features (distance to the city, suburb, number of rooms, land size, etc.) as independent variables and the selling price of other houses in the neighborhood as the dependent variable to design a prediction model. The prediction model can then predict the value (y) of a house with an unknown selling price by inputting its features (X) into the prediction model.

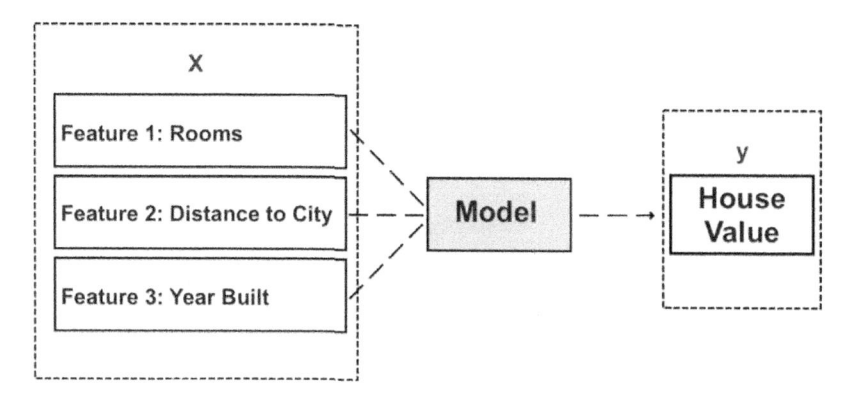

Figure 1: House value prediction model

Supervised, Unsupervised & Reinforcement Learning

Self-learning can be divided into three categories: supervised, unsupervised, and reinforcement.

Supervised learning decodes known relationships between independent variables and the dependent variable. This involves feeding the machine sample data with various features (X) and their known output value (y). The fact that the input and output values are known qualifies the dataset as "labeled" or "supervised." The algorithm deciphers patterns that exist in the dataset and creates a model that interprets new data based on the underlying rules of the labeled data.

The house model mentioned earlier is a typical example of supervised learning in which a set of input features (i.e. rooms, distance to the city, etc.) are analyzed in response to their labeled output (house value) across many examples to build a prediction model. Using rules learned from the existing data, the model is then able to predict the output of new data based on the input features.

In the case of *unsupervised learning*, the dependent variables aren't known or labeled and the model looks at patterns among independent variables to create a new output. In the case of clustering analysis, this can be achieved by grouping similar data points and finding connections that generalize patterns, such as the grouping of suburbs with two-bedroom apartments that generate a high property valuation. In the case of *dimensionality reduction*, the goal of unsupervised learning is to create an output with fewer dimensions (features) than the original input data.

As there are no known output observations available to check and validate the model, there is no true output in unsupervised learning and predictions are more subjective than that of supervised learning.

Unsupervised learning is useful in situations where there's no single clear prediction goal and exploratory data analysis is required to uncover new categories and subgroups. Unsupervised learning is also useful for taking complex unlabeled data with a high number of variables and transforming that data into a low number of synthesized variables that are plottable on a 2-D or 3-D plot as output. Although the input data has been transformed, the goal is to preserve as much of the data's original structure as possible, allowing you to better understand the structure of the data and identify unsuspected patterns.[6]

---

[6] Aurélien Géron, "Hands-On Machine Learning with Scikit-Learn and TensorFlow: Concepts, Tools, and Techniques to Build Intelligent Systems," *O'Reilly Media*, 2017.

Other popular unsupervised learning tasks include anomaly detection such as fraudulent transactions or catching manufacturing defects, and automatically removing outliers and complexity from a dataset before feeding the data to a supervised learning algorithm.

Reinforcement learning is the third and most advanced category of machine learning and is generally used for performing a sequence of decisions, such as playing chess or driving an automobile.

Reinforcement learning is the opposite of unsupervised learning as the output (y) is known but the inputs (X) are unknown. The output can be considered as the intended goal (i.e. win a game of chess) and the optimal input is found using a brute force technique based on trial and error. Random input data is fed to the model and graded according to its relationship to the target output. In the case of self-driving vehicles, movements to avoid a crash are graded positively, and in the case of chess, moves to avoid defeat are rewarded. Over time, the model leverages this feedback to progressively improve its choice of input variables to achieve its desired output goal.

The AI company Wayve has released a live video recording of a car learning to drive, which demonstrates the random and iterative nature of reinforcement learning. Using sensors and a safety driver who intervenes when the car drifts off-course, the car learns to navigate the circuit within just 20 minutes of training.

Video link: http://bit.ly/2YZHaLS

QUIZ

1) A model that predicts the height of adult students based on the height of their adult relatives is an example of:

a. Supervised learning
b. Unsupervised learning
c. Reinforcement learning
d. Classification

2) What type of machine learning model is most likely to perform a never-seen-before move in a video game to defeat its human opponent?

a. Supervised learning
b. Unsupervised learning
c. Extra supervised learning
d. Reinforcement learning

3) What type of machine learning model can we use to filter customers into unlabeled groups based <u>only</u> on known inputs such as age, average spending amount, and nationality?

a. Supervised learning
b. Unsupervised learning
c. Reinforcement learning
d. Extra supervised learning

4) Arthur Samuel's checkers program is an example of:

a. Supervised learning
b. Unsupervised learning
c. Reinforcement learning
d. Extra supervised learning

5) Which is not an example of an independent variable for predicting house prices as part of a supervised learning model?

a. Distance to city
b. Year built
c. Suburb
d. Price of house

SOLUTIONS

1) a, Supervised learning

2) d, Reinforcement learning

3) b, Unsupervised learning

4) a, Supervised learning

5) d, Price of house

2

DEVELOPMENT ENVIRONMENT

As the practical exercises delivered in this book use Jupyter Notebook as the development environment for Python 3, this chapter serves as an optional guide for installing Jupyter Notebook. If you have prior experience using Jupyter Notebook or have read my earlier title Machine Learning for Absolute Beginners, then you may wish to proceed to the next chapter.

Jupyter Notebook is a popular choice for practitioners and online courses alike, as it combines live code, explanatory notes, and visualizations into one convenient workspace and runs from any web browser.

Jupyter Notebook can be installed using the Anaconda Distribution or Python's package manager, pip. As an experienced Python user, you may wish to install Jupyter Notebook via pip, and there are instructions available on the Jupyter Notebook website (http://jupyter.org/install.html) outlining this option. For beginners, I recommend choosing the Anaconda Distribution option, which offers an easy click-and-drag setup (https://www.anaconda.com/distribution/). This installation option will direct you to the Anaconda website. From there, you can select your preferred installation for Windows, macOS, or Linux. Again, you can find instructions available on the Anaconda website based on your operating system.

After installing Anaconda on your machine, you'll have access to a number of data science applications including rstudio, Jupyter Notebook, and graphviz for data visualization through the

Anaconda application. Next, you need to select Jupyter Notebook by clicking on "Launch" inside the Jupyter Notebook tab.

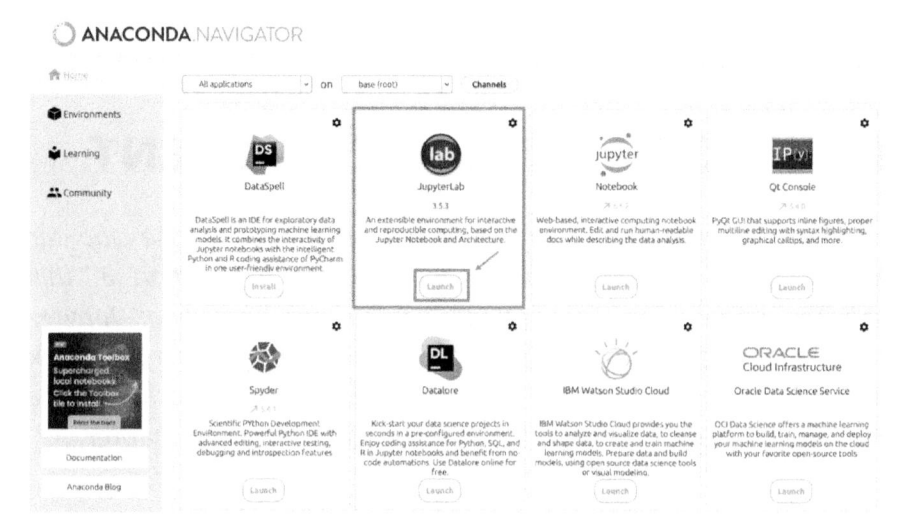

Figure 2: The Anaconda Navigator portal

To initiate Jupyter Notebook, run the following command from the Terminal (for Mac/Linux) or Command Prompt (for Windows):

```
jupyter notebook
```

Terminal/Command Prompt then generates a URL for you to copy and paste it into your web browser.

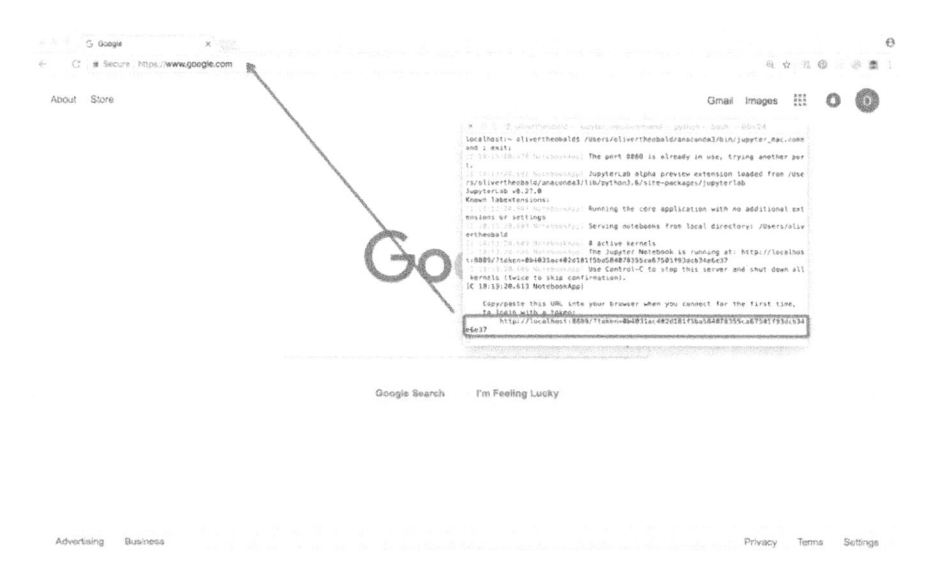

Figure 3: Copy URL and paste it into your browser

Copy and paste the generated URL into your browser to access Jupyter Notebook. Once you have Jupyter Notebook open in your browser, click on "New" in the top right-hand corner of the web application to create a new notebook project, and select "Python 3."

Figure 4: Inside Jupyter Notebook

You've now successfully set up a sandbox environment in your web browser using Jupyter Notebook. This means that the following experimentation and code changes will not affect resources outside of the isolated testing environment.

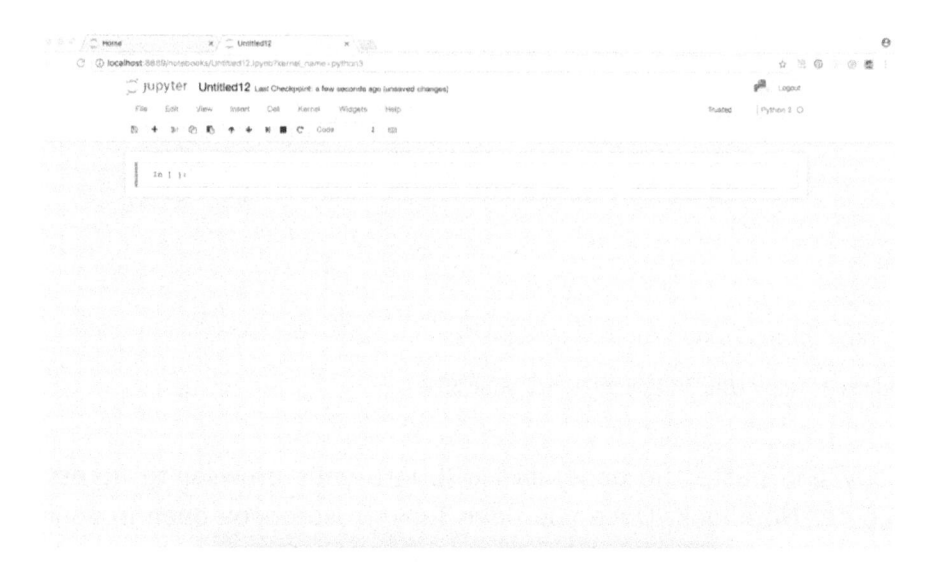

Figure 5: A new Jupyter notebook ready for coding

3

MACHINE LEARNING LIBRARIES

Data scientists rarely work alone. This means it's vital to maintain consistent code that can be read and reused by other programmers. Similar to using WordPress plugins with websites, code libraries makes it easy for data scientists to perform common tasks using pre-written modules of code.

With WordPress, for example, you can install a comments management plugin called Discuz on a portfolio of websites. Using the same plugin for each website eliminates the need for developers to familiarize themselves with each site's underlying code. They simply need to familiarize themselves with the basic interface and customization settings of the Discuz plugin.

The same logic and benefits apply to machine learning libraries, as complex algorithms and other functions can be called through the same code interface. Moreover, rather than writing the statistical requirements of a regression algorithm over many lines of code, you can call the algorithm from a library such as Scikit-learn using just one line of code.

Example:

```
my_model = LinearRegression()
```

The libraries themselves are imported on a project-by-project basis according to the scope of your project, i.e. data visualization, deep learning, exploratory data analysis, shallow algorithms, data scrubbing, decision tree flow maps, ensemble modeling using multiple algorithm types, etc.

The remainder of this chapter provides a brief rundown of the most popular Python libraries used within machine learning.

Pandas

Pandas is a library for managing and presenting your data. The name "Pandas" comes from the term "panel data," which refers to Panda's ability to create a series of panels, similar to sheets in Excel.

Pandas can be used to organize structured data as a dataframe, which is a two-dimensional data structure (tabular dataset) with labeled rows and columns, similar to a spreadsheet or SQL table. You can also use Pandas to import and manipulate an external dataset including CSV files as a dataframe without affecting the source file as modifications take place inside your development environment.

	Suburb	Address	Rooms	Type	Price	Method	SellerG	Date	Distance	Postcode	...	Bathroom	Car	Landsize	BuildingArea	YearBuilt
0	Abbotsford	68 Studley St	2	h	NaN	SS	Jellis	3/09/2016	2.5	3067.0	...	1.0	1.0	126.0	NaN	NaN
1	Abbotsford	85 Turner St	2	h	1480000.0	S	Biggin	3/12/2016	2.5	3067.0	...	1.0	1.0	202.0	NaN	NaN
2	Abbotsford	25 Bloomburg St	2	h	1035000.0	S	Biggin	4/02/2016	2.5	3067.0	...	1.0	0.0	156.0	79.0	1900.0
3	Abbotsford	18/659 Victoria St	3	u	NaN	VB	Rounds	4/02/2016	2.5	3067.0	...	2.0	1.0	0.0	NaN	NaN
4	Abbotsford	5 Charles St	3	h	1465000.0	SP	Biggin	4/03/2017	2.5	3067.0	...	2.0	0.0	134.0	150.0	1900.0

Figure 6: Example of a Pandas' dataframe

NumPy

NumPy is often used in combination with Pandas and is short for "numeric Python." On its own, NumPy is used for managing multi-dimensional arrays and matrices, merging and slicing datasets, and offers a collection of mathematical functions including min, max, mean, standard deviation, and variance.

NumPy consumes less memory and is said to perform better than Pandas with 50,000 rows or less.[7] NumPy, though, is often used

---

[7] Goutham Balaraman, "NumPy Vs Pandas Performance Comparison," *gouthamanbalaraman.com*,

in conjunction with Pandas as the latter is more user-friendly and easier to interpret in an interactive environment such as Jupyter Notebook. A Pandas dataframe is also more suitable for managing a mix of data types, whereas a NumPy array is designed for dealing with numerical data, especially multi-dimensional data.[8]

Most machine learning models demonstrated to beginners in massive open online courses and textbooks structure data as a Pandas dataframe rather than a NumPy array but often draw on the NumPy library for mathematical and other miscellaneous operations.

Scikit-learn

Scikit-learn is the core library for general machine learning. It offers an extensive repository of shallow algorithms[9] including logistic regression, decision trees, linear regression, gradient boosting, etc., a broad range of evaluation metrics such as mean absolute error, as well as data partition methods including split validation and cross validation.

Scikit-learn is also used to perform a number of important machine learning tasks including training the model and using the trained model to predict the test data.

The following table is a brief overview of common terms and functions used in machine learning from Scikit-learn.

March 14, 2017, http://gouthamanbalaraman.com/blog/numpy-vs-pandas-comparison.html

[8] Dimensions are the number of variables characterizing the data, such as the city of residence, country of residence, age, and sex of a user. Up to four variables can be plotted on a scatterplot but three-dimensional and two-dimensional plots are easier for human eyes to interpret.

[9] Shallow algorithms can be roughly characterized as non-deep learning approaches that aren't structured as part of a sophisticated network. In shallow learning, the model predicts outcomes directly from the input features, whereas in deep learning, the output is based on the output of preceding layers in the model and not directly from the input features.

Term	Explanation	Code Example
| estimator | An estimator refers to a set hyperparameter value, such as C in Support Vector Machines, n neighbors in k-NN or n number of trees in random forests. Set prior to training your model, the estimator maps each hyperparameter value to the learning algorithm. | ```
model = ensemble.GradientBoostingRegressor(
    n_estimators = 150,
    learning_rate = 0.1,
    max_depth = 30,
    min_samples_split = 4,
    min_samples_leaf = 6,
    max_features = 0.6,
    loss = 'huber'
)
```  Each of the seven hyperparameters represents an individual estimator for the algorithm gradient boosting. |
| fit() | After setting the estimator(s), the fit() function is used to run the learning algorithm on the training data and train the prediction model. | ```
model = KNeighborsClassifier(n_neighbors=5)
model.fit(X_train, y_train)
```  This code excerpt fits the k-NN model to the X and y training data. |
| predict() | After the model has been trained, the predict() function uses the newly trained model to make predictions using the X test data. In the case of supervised learning, this involves using the model to predict the labels or values of the X test data. | ```
prediction = model.predict(X_test)
```  In this example, the trained model is asked to predict the X test data and is assigned as a new variable ("prediction"). |
| transform() | The transform() function is used to modify the data before feeding it to a learning algorithm (pre-processing). This means taking the original data and outputting a transformed version of it. Examples include normalization, standardization, dimensionality reduction. | ```
from sklearn.preprocessing import StandardScaler
scaler = StandardScaler()
scaler.fit(X_train)
X_train = scaler.transform(X_train)
```  After importing StandardScaler, we can use the transform method to rescale/standardize the X training data. The transformed training data is scaled to unit variance with a mean of zero and can now be fit to a learning algorithm. |

Table 1: Overview of key Scikit-learn terms and functions

Matplotlib

Matplotlib is a visualization library you can use to generate scatterplots, histograms, pie charts, bar charts, error charts, and other visual charts with just a few lines of code. While Matplotlib offers detailed manual control over line styles, font properties, colors, axes, and properties, the default visual presentation is not as striking and professional as other visualization libraries and is generally used in conjunction with Seaborn themes.

Seaborn

Seaborn is a popular Python visualization library based on Matplotlib. This library comes with numerous built-in themes for visualization and complex visual techniques including color visualization of dependent and independent variables, sophisticated heatmaps, cluster maps, and pairplots. The combination of Seaborn's pre-formatted visual design and Matplotlib's customizability make it easy to generate publication-quality visualizations.

Other popular visualization libraries include Plotly (an interactive visualization Python library) and Cufflinks (which connects Plotly directly with Pandas dataframes to create graphs and charts).

TensorFlow

A round-up of popular machine learning libraries wouldn't be complete without an introduction to Google's TensorFlow. While Scikit-learn offers a broad set of popular shallow algorithms, TensorFlow is the library of choice for deep learning and artificial neural networks (ANN).

TensorFlow was created at Google and supports various advanced distributed numerical computation techniques. By distributing computations on a network with up to thousands of GPU instances, TensorFlow supports advanced algorithms including neural networks that would be impossible to run on a single server.

Unfortunately for Mac users, TensorFlow is only compatible with the Nvidia GPU card, which is no longer available with Mac OS X. Mac users can still run TensorFlow on their CPU but will need to run their workload on the cloud to access the GPU.

QUIZ

1) Which library is better for managing a mix of data types (numeric and non-numerical data)?

a. NumPy
b. Pandas
c. Seaborn
d. Matplotlib

2) Which Python library should we use for importing common shallow algorithms?

a. Scikit-learn
b. Pandas
c. Tensorflow
d. Seaborn

3) Which Python libraries can be used for visualizing data relationships?

a. Scikit-learn
b. Cuffles-learn
c. Matplotlib
d. Seaborn

4) Which of the following is a dataframe?

a. A NumPy data structure
b. A Pandas data structure
c. A Scikit-learn function
d. An Excel pivot table

5) Tensorflow is generally used for deep learning. True or False?

SOLUTIONS

1) b, Pandas

2) a, Scikit-learn

3) c & d, Matplotlib and Seaborn

4) b, A Pandas data structure

5) True

4

EXPLORATORY DATA ANALYSIS

In this chapter, we introduce managing data as a Pandas dataframe and common exploratory data analysis (EDA) techniques.

As a key part of data inspection, EDA involves summarizing the salient characteristics of your dataset in preparation for further processing and analysis. This includes understanding the shape and distribution of the data, scanning for missing values, learning which features are most relevant based on correlation, and familiarizing yourself with the overall contents of the dataset. Gathering this intel helps to inform algorithm selection and highlight parts of the data that require cleaning in preparation for further processing.

Using Pandas, there's a range of simple techniques we can use to summarize data and additional options to visualize the data using Seaborn and Matplotlib.

Let's begin by importing Pandas, Seaborn, and Matplotlib inline using the following code in Jupyter Notebook.

```
import pandas as pd
import seaborn as sns
%matplotlib inline
```

Note that using the `inline` feature of Matplotlib, we can display plots directly below the applicable code cell within Jupyter Notebook or other frontends.

Import Dataset

Datasets can be imported from a variety of sources, including internal and external files as well as random self-generated datasets called *blobs*.

The following sample dataset is an external dataset downloaded from Kaggle.com, called the Berlin Airbnb dataset. This data was scraped from airbnb.com and contains detailed listings of accommodation available in Berlin, including location, price, and reviews.

Feature	Data Type	Continuous/Discrete
id	Integer	Discrete
name	String	Discrete
host_id	Integer	Discrete
host_name	String	Discrete
neighbourhood_group	String	Discrete
neighbourhood	String	Discrete
latitude	String	Discrete
longitude	String	Discrete
room_type	String	Discrete
price	Integer	Continuous
minimum_nights	Integer	Continuous
number_of_reviews	Integer	Continuous
last_review	TimeDate	Discrete
reviews_per_month	Floating-point	Continuous
calculated_host_listings_count	Integer	Continuous
availability_365	Integer	Continuous

Table 2: Overview of the Berlin Airbnb dataset

The dataset can be downloaded from the following link: http://bit.ly/2YPwUdl

After registering a free account and logging into kaggle.com, download the dataset as a zip file. Next, unzip the downloaded file called listings.csv and import it into Jupyter Notebook as a Pandas dataframe using `pd.read_csv`.

```
# For Mac users
df = pd.read_csv('~/Downloads/listings.csv')
```

Keep in mind that you'll need to assign a variable name to store the dataset for ongoing reference. Common variable names for dataframes are "df" or "dataframe," but you can also choose another variable name that complies with the naming of variables in Python.[10] In this book, we use "df" as the variable name for dataframes.

Please also note that the file path of your dataset will vary depending on its saved location and your computer's operating system. If saved to Desktop on Windows, you would import the .csv file using a structure similar to this example:

```
# For Windows users
df = pd.read_csv('C:\Users\John\Desktop\listings.csv')
```

As the backward slash is used as the 'escape' character in Python, you may need to add the "r" prefix to your pathname to indicate a "raw" string of text.

```
# For Windows users
df = pd.read_csv(r'C:\Users\John\Desktop\listings.csv')
```

Documentation for Read_CSV: http://bit.ly/2H1UNnP

Preview the Dataframe

We can now use the Pandas' `head()` command to preview the dataframe in Jupyter Notebook. The `head()` function must come after the variable name of the dataframe, which in this case is `df`.

---

[10] Information regarding variable naming conditions in Python can be located in Appendix 1 of this book.

`df.head()`

To preview the dataframe, run the code by using right-click and selecting "Run" or navigating from the Jupyter Notebook menu: Cell > Run All

Figure 7: Run All from the navigation menu

After the code has run, Pandas will populate the imported dataset as a dataframe as shown in the next screenshot.

Figure 8: Previewing a dataframe in Jupyter Notebook using head()

35

Notice that the first row (id 2015, located in Mitte) is indexed at position 0 of the dataframe. The fifth row, meanwhile, is indexed at position 4. The indexing of elements in Python starts at 0, which means you will need to subtract 1 from the actual number of rows when calling a specific row from the dataframe.

The dataframe's columns, while not labeled numerically, follow the same logic. The first column **(id)** is indexed at 0 and the fifth column (**neighbourhood_group**) is indexed at 4. This is a fixed feature of working in Python and something to keep in mind when calling specific rows or columns.

By default, `head()` displays the first five rows of the dataframe, but you can increase the number of rows by specifying *n* number of rows inside parentheses, as demonstrated in Figure 9.

```
5  df = pd.read_csv('~/Downloads/listings.csv')
6
7  df.head(10)
```

	id	name	host_id	host_name	neighbourhood_group	neighbourhood	latitude	longitude	room_type	price	minimum_nights
0	2015	Berlin-Mitte Value! Quiet courtyard/very central	2217	Ian	Mitte	Brunnenstr. Süd	52.534537	13.402557	Entire home/apt	60	4
1	2695	Prenzlauer Berg close to Mauerpark	2986	Michael	Pankow	Prenzlauer Berg Nordwest	52.548513	13.404553	Private room	17	2
2	3176	Fabulous Flat in great Location	3718	Britta	Pankow	Prenzlauer Berg Südwest	52.534996	13.417579	Entire home/apt	90	62
3	3309	BerlinSpot Schöneberg near KaDeWe	4108	Jana	Tempelhof - Schöneberg	Schöneberg-Nord	52.498855	13.349065	Private room	26	5
4	7071	BrightRoom with sunny greenview!	17391	Bright	Pankow	Helmholtzplatz	52.543157	13.415091	Private room	42	2
5	9991	Geourgeous flat - outstanding views	33852	Philipp	Pankow	Prenzlauer Berg Südwest	52.533031	13.416047	Entire home/apt	180	6
6	14325	Apartment in Prenzlauer Berg	55531	Chris + Oliver	Pankow	Prenzlauer Berg Nordwest	52.547846	13.405562	Entire home/apt	70	90
7	16401	APARTMENT TO RENT	59666	Melanie	Friedrichshain-Kreuzberg	Frankfurter Allee Süd FK	52.510514	13.457850	Private room	120	30
8	16644	In the Heart of Berlin - Kreuzberg	64696	Rene	Friedrichshain-Kreuzberg	nördliche Luisenstadt	52.504792	13.435102	Entire home/apt	90	60
9	17409	Downtown Above The Roofs In	67590	Wolfram	Pankow	Prenzlauer Berg Südwest	52.529071	13.412843	Private room	45	3

Figure 9: Previewing the first ten rows of a dataframe

The argument `head(10)` is used to preview the first ten rows of the dataframe. You can also view columns concealed to the right by scrolling to the right inside Jupyter Notebook. Regarding rows, you can only preview the number of rows specified in the code. Lastly, you will sometimes see `n=` inserted inside `head()`, which is an alternative method to specify *n* number of previewed rows.

Example code:

```
df.head(n=10)
```

Documentation for Dataframe Head: http://bit.ly/2ZQxIvy

Dataframe Tail

The inverse operation of `head()` and previewing the top *n* rows of the dataframe is the `tail()` method, which displays the bottom *n* rows of the dataframe. Below, we can see an example of previewing the dataframe using `tail()`, which also by default displays five rows. Again, you will need to run the code to view the output.

```
1  import pandas as pd
2  import seaborn as sns
3  %matplotlib inline
4
5  df = pd.read_csv('~/Downloads/listings.csv')
6
7  df.tail()
```

	id	name	host_id	host_name	neighbourhood group	neighbourhood	latitude	longitude	room_type	price	minimum_nights
22547	29856708	Cozy Apartment right in the center of Berlin	87555909	Ulisses	Mitte	Brunnenstr. Süd	52.533865	13.400731	Entire home/apt	60	2
22548	29857106	Altbau/ Schöneberger Kiez / Schlafsofa	67537363	Jörg	Tempelhof - Schöneberg	Schöneberg-Nord	52.496211	13.341738	Shared room	20	1
22549	29864272	Artists loft with garden in the center of Berlin	3146923	Martin	Pankow	Prenzlauer Berg Südwest	52.531800	13.411999	Entire home/apt	85	3
22550	29866805	Room for two with private shower / WC	36961901	Arte Luise	Mitte	Alexanderplatz	52.520802	13.378688	Private room	99	1
22551	29867352	Sunny, modern and cozy flat in Berlin Neukölln :)	177464875	Sebastian	Neukölln	Schillerpromenade	52.473762	13.424447	Private room	45	5

Figure 10: Previewing the last five rows of a dataframe using tail()

Documentation for Dataframe Tail: http://bit.ly/2McjqCa

Shape

A quick method to inspect the size of the dataframe is the `shape` method, which returns the number of rows and columns contained in the dataframe. This is useful because the size of the dataset is likely to change as you remove missing values, transform features or delete features.

To query the number of rows and columns in the dataframe, you can use the `shape` method preceded by the name of the dataset (parentheses are not used with this method).

`df.shape`

```
1  import pandas as pd
2  import seaborn as sns
3  %matplotlib inline
4
5  df = pd.read_csv('~/Downloads/listings.csv')
6
7  df.shape
```
(22552, 16)

Figure 11: Inspecting the shape (number of rows and columns) of the dataframe

In the case of this dataframe, there are 22,552 rows and 16 columns.

Columns

Another useful method is `columns`, which prints the dataframe's column titles. This is useful for copying and pasting columns back into the code or clarifying the name of specific variables.

`df.columns`

```
1  import pandas as pd
2  import seaborn as sns
3  %matplotlib inline
4
5  df = pd.read_csv('~/Downloads/listings.csv')
6
7  df.columns
```

```
Index(['id', 'name', 'host_id', 'host_name', 'neighbourhood_group',
       'neighbourhood', 'latitude', 'longitude', 'room_type', 'price',
       'minimum_nights', 'number_of_reviews', 'last_review',
       'reviews_per_month', 'calculated_host_listings_count',
       'availability_365'],
      dtype='object')
```

Figure 12: Print columns

Describe

The `describe()` method is convenient for generating a summary of the dataframe's mean, standard deviation, and IQR (interquartile range) values. Note that this method performs optimally with continuous values (integers or floating-point numbers that can be easily aggregated).

`df.describe()`

```
1  import pandas as pd
2  import seaborn as sns
3  %matplotlib inline
4
5  df = pd.read_csv('~/Downloads/listings.csv')
6
7  df.describe()
```

	id	host_id	latitude	longitude	price	minimum_nights	number_of_reviews	reviews_per_month	calculated_host_listing
count	2.255200e+04	2.255200e+04	22552.000000	22552.000000	22552.000000	22552.000000	22552.000000	18636.000000	22552
mean	1.571560e+07	5.403355e+07	52.509824	13.406107	67.143668	7.157059	17.840679	1.135525	1
std	8.552069e+06	5.816290e+07	0.030825	0.057964	220.266210	40.665073	36.769624	1.507082	3
min	2.015000e+03	2.217000e+03	52.345803	13.103557	0.000000	1.000000	0.000000	0.010000	1
25%	8.065954e+06	9.240002e+06	52.489065	13.375411	30.000000	2.000000	1.000000	0.180000	1
50%	1.686638e+07	3.126711e+07	52.509079	13.416279	45.000000	2.000000	5.000000	0.540000	1
75%	2.258393e+07	8.067518e+07	52.532669	13.439259	70.000000	4.000000	16.000000	1.500000	1
max	2.986735e+07	2.245061e+08	52.651670	13.757642	9000.000000	5000.000000	498.000000	36.670000	45

Figure 13: Using the describe method to summarize the dataframe

By default, `describe()` excludes columns that contain non-numeric values and instead provides a statistical summary of those columns that do contain numeric values. However, it's also possible to run this method on non-numerical values by adding

39

the argument `include='all'` within parentheses to obtain the summary statistics of both numeric and non-numeric columns (where applicable).

```
df.describe(include='all')
```

```
1  import pandas as pd
2  import seaborn as sns
3  %matplotlib inline
4
5  df = pd.read_csv('~/Downloads/listings.csv')
6
7  df.describe(include='all')
```

	id	name	host id	host name	neighbourhood group	neighbourhood	latitude	longitude	room type	price	minimu
count	2.255200e+04	22493	2.255200e+04	22526	22552	22552	22552.000000	22552.000000	22552	22552.000000	225
unique	NaN	21873	NaN	5997	12	136	NaN	NaN	3	NaN	
top	NaN	Berlin Wohnung	NaN	Anna	Friedrichshain-Kreuzberg	Tempelhofer Vorstadt	NaN	NaN	Private room	NaN	
freq	NaN	14	NaN	216	5497	1325	NaN	NaN	11534	NaN	
mean	1.571560e+07	NaN	5.403355e+07	NaN	NaN	NaN	52.509824	13.406107	NaN	67.143668	
std	8.552069e+06	NaN	5.816290e+07	NaN	NaN	NaN	0.030825	0.057964	NaN	220.266210	
min	2.015000e+03	NaN	2.217000e+03	NaN	NaN	NaN	52.345803	13.103557	NaN	0.000000	
25%	8.065954e+06	NaN	9.240002e+06	NaN	NaN	NaN	52.489065	13.375411	NaN	30.000000	
50%	1.686638e+07	NaN	3.126711e+07	NaN	NaN	NaN	52.509079	13.416779	NaN	45.000000	
75%	2.258393e+07	NaN	8.067518e+07	NaN	NaN	NaN	52.532669	13.439259	NaN	70.000000	
max	2.988735e+07	NaN	2.245081e+08	NaN	NaN	NaN	52.651670	13.757642	NaN	9000.000000	50

Figure 14: All variables added to the description

Having consolidated methods to inspect and query the size of the dataframe using Pandas, we'll now move on to generating visual summaries of the data using Seaborn and Matplotlib.

Documentation for Describe: http://bit.ly/31BVQ5L

Pairplots

One of the most popular exploratory techniques for understanding patterns between two variables is the pairplot. A pairplot takes the form of a 2-D or 3-D grid of plots that display variables against other variables taken from the dataframe as shown in Figure 15.

```
sns.pairplot(df,vars=['price','number_of_reviews','availability_365'])
```

```
1  import pandas as pd
2  import seaborn as sns
3  %matplotlib inline
4
5  df = pd.read_csv('~/Downloads/listings.csv')
6  sns.pairplot(df,vars=['price','number_of_reviews','availability_365'])
7
```

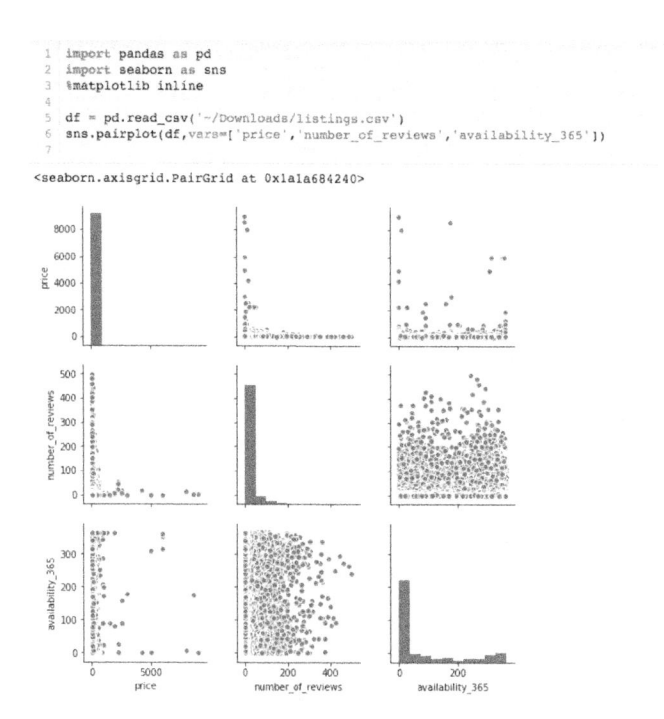

<seaborn.axisgrid.PairGrid at 0x1a1a684240>

Figure 15: Example of a pairplot grid based on three chosen variables

Using `pairplot` from Seaborn, we've plotted three chosen variables against each other, which helps us to understand the relationships and variance between those variables. When plotted against other variables (multivariant), the visualization takes the form of a scatterplot, and when plotted against the same variable (univariant), a simple histogram is generated.

Documentation for Seaborn Pairplot: http://bit.ly/2McQASq

Heatmaps

Heatmaps are also useful for inspecting and understanding relationships between variables. The variables are structured as both columns and rows on a matrix, with individual values represented as colors on a heatmap.

We can build a heatmap in Python using the `corr` (correlation) function from Pandas and then visualize the results using a Seaborn heatmap.

```
df_corr = df.corr()

sns.heatmap(df_corr,annot=True,cmap='coolwarm')
```

```
10  df_corr = df.corr()
11  sns.heatmap(df_corr,annot=True,cmap='coolwarm')
12
```

<matplotlib.axes._subplots.AxesSubplot at 0x1a1f25bc18>

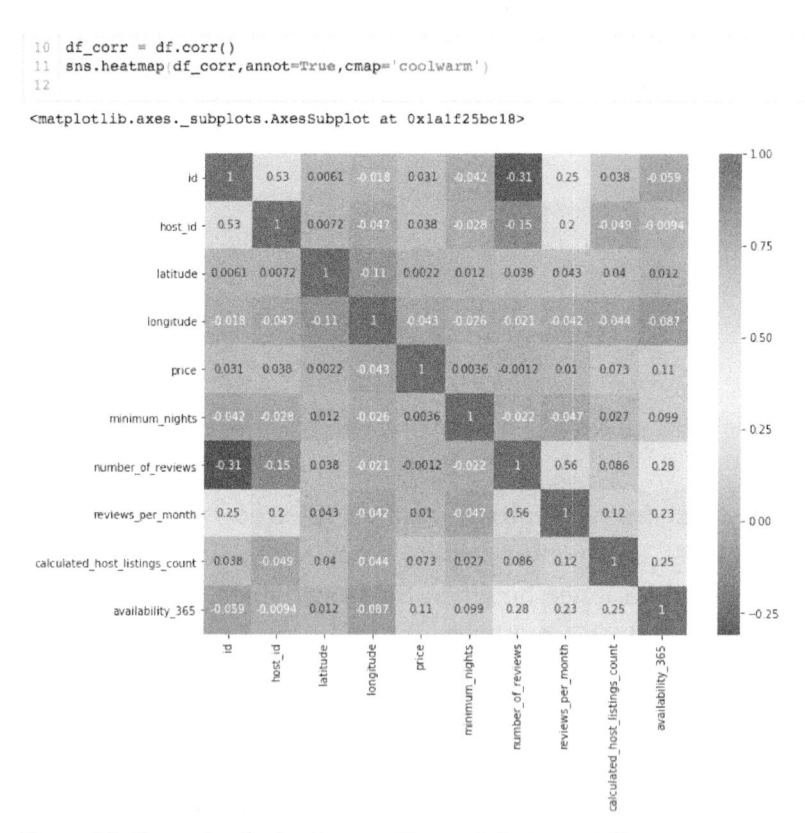

Figure 16: Example of a heatmap with annotated correlation scores

Documentation for Seaborn Heatmaps: http://bit.ly/2yShE0I

QUIZ

1) Which method can we use to view the bottom *n* rows of a Pandas dataframe?

a. head()
b. tail()
c. describe()
d. columns

2) Which method can we use to view the top *n* rows of a Pandas dataframe?

a. head()
b. tail()
c. describe()
d. columns

3) Which method can we use to generate a summary of the dataframe's mean, standard deviation, and IQR values?

a. head()
b. tail()
c. describe()
d. columns

4) Which technique is not an example of exploratory data visualization?

a. heatmap
b. pairplot
c. shape
d. scatterplot

5) Which code command can we use to preview a Pandas dataframe (df) inside a notebook?

a. df.head()
b. df_head()
c. df.header()
d. df.shape()

SOLUTIONS

1) b, tail()

2) a, head()

3) c, describe()

4) c, shape

5) a, df.head()

5

DATA SCRUBBING

Similar to Swiss or Japanese watch design, a good machine learning model should run smoothly and contain no extra parts. This means avoiding syntax or other errors that prevent the code from executing and removing redundant variables that might clog up the model's decision path.

This inclination towards simplicity extends to beginners coding their first model. When working with a new algorithm, it helps to create a minimal viable model and add complexity to the code later. If you find yourself at an impasse, look at the troublesome element and ask, *"Do I need it?"* If the model can't handle missing values or multiple variable types, the quickest cure is to remove those variables. This should help the afflicted model spring to life and breathe normally. Once the model is working, you can go back and add complexity to your code.

Let's now take a look at specific data scrubbing techniques to prepare, streamline, and optimize the data for analysis.

What is Data Scrubbing?

Data scrubbing is an umbrella term for manipulating data in preparation for analysis. Some algorithms, for example, don't recognize specific data types or return an error message in response to missing values or non-numeric input. Variables, too, may need to be scaled to size or converted to a more compatible data type. Linear regression, for example, analyzes continuous variables, whereas gradient boosting asks that both discrete (categorical) and continuous variables are expressed numerically as an integer or floating-point number.

Duplicate information, redundant variables, and errors in the data are other problems that often conspire to derail the model's capacity to dispense valuable insight. Another potential consideration when working with data, and specifically private data, is removing personal identifiers that could contravene relevant data privacy regulations or damage the trust of customers, users, and other stakeholders. This is less of a problem for publicly available datasets but something to be mindful of when working with private data.

Removing Variables

Preparing the data for further processing generally starts with removing variables that aren't compatible with the chosen algorithm or variables that are deemed less relevant to your target output. Determining which variables to remove from the dataset is assessed using exploratory data analysis and domain knowledge.

In regards to exploratory data analysis, checking the data type of your variables (i.e. string, Boolean, integer, etc.) and the correlation between variables is a useful measure to eliminate variables.[11] Domain knowledge, meanwhile, is useful for spotting duplicate variables such as country and country code, and eliminating less relevant variables like latitude and longitude, for example.

In Python, variables can be removed from the dataframe using the `del` function alongside the variable name of the dataframe and the title of the column you wish to remove. The column title should be nested inside quotation marks and square brackets as shown here.

```
del df['latitude']
```

---

[11] Conversely, exploratory analysis of variables may impact the choice of algorithm, i.e. matching a flexible algorithm like gradient boosting or random forests to a mix of data types.

```
del df['longitude']
```

Note that this code example, in addition to other changes made inside your notebook, won't affect or alter the source file of the dataset. You can even restore variables removed from the development environment by deleting the relevant line(s) of code. In fact, it's common to reverse the removal of features when testing the model using different combinations of variables.

One-hot Encoding

In data science, it's common to have a mismatch or compatibility issue between the data and the algorithm. While the contents of the variable might be relevant, the algorithm might not be able to read the data in its default form. Text-based categorical values, for example, can't be parsed and mathematically modeled using general clustering and regression algorithms.

One quick remedy is to re-express categorical variables as a numeric categorizer. This can be performed using a common technique called one-hot encoding that converts categorical variables into binary form, represented as "1" or "0"—"True" or "False."

```
import pandas as pd
df = pd.read_csv('~/Downloads/listings.csv')
df = pd.get_dummies(df, columns = ['neighbourhood_group', 'neighbourhood'])
df.head()
```

Run the code in Jupyter Notebook.

```
import pandas as pd
df = pd.read_csv('~/Downloads/listings.csv')
df = pd.get_dummies(df, columns = ['neighbourhood_group', 'neighbourhood'])
df.head()
```

neighbourhood_West_3	neighbourhood_West_4	neighbourhood_West_5	neighbourhood_Westend	neighbourhood_Wiesbadener Straße
0	0	0	0	0
0	0	0	0	0
0	0	0	0	0
0	0	0	0	0
0	0	0	0	0

Figure 17: Example of one-hot encoding

One-hot encoding expands the dataframe horizontally with the addition of new columns. While expanding the dataset isn't a major issue, you can simplify the dataframe and enjoy faster processing speed using a parameter to remove expendable columns. Using the logic of deduction, this parameter reduces one column for each original variable. To illustrate this concept, consider the following example:

	gender_male	gender_female	city_london	city_mumbai	city_tokyo
Sam	1	0	1	0	0
Rahul	1	0	0	1	0
Mariko	0	1	0	0	1

Table 3: Original dataframe

	gender_male	city_london	city_mumbai
Sam	1	1	0
Rahul	1	0	1
Mariko	0	0	0

Table 4: Simplified dataframe with dropped columns

While it appears that information has been removed from the second dataframe, the Python interpreter can deduct the true value of each variable without referring to the expendable (removed) columns. In the case of Mariko, the Python interpreter can deduct that the subject is from Tokyo based on the false argument of the other two variables. In statistics, this concept is known as *multi-collinearity* and describes the ability to predict a variable based on the value of other variables.

To remove expendable columns in Python we can add the parameter `drop_first=True`, which removes the first column for each variable.

```
df = pd.get_dummies(df, columns = ['neighbourhood_group',
'neighbourhood'] , drop_first = True)
```

Drop Missing Values

Another common but more complicated problem is deciding what to do with missing data. Missing data can be split into three categories: missing completely at random (MCAR), missing at random (MAR), and nonignorable.

MCAR occurs when there's no relationship between a missing value and other values in the dataset. Oftentimes, the value is not readily available and is therefore left out of the dataset.

Missing at random means the missing value is not related to its own value but to the values of other variables. In census surveys, for example, a respondent might skip an extended response question because relevant information was inputted in a previous question, or alternatively, they fail to complete the census survey due to low levels of language proficiency as stated by the respondent elsewhere in the survey (i.e. a question about the respondent's level of English fluency). In other words, the reason why the value is missing is linked to another variable in the dataset and not due directly to the value itself.

Lastly, nonignorable missing data constitutes the absence of data due directly to its own value or significance of the information. Tax evading citizens or respondents with a criminal record may decline to supply information to certain questions due to feelings of sensitivity towards that question, for example.

The irony of these three categories is that because the data is missing, it's difficult to diagnose why the data is missing. Problem-solving skills and awareness of these three categories can help to diagnose and correct the root cause for missing values. This might include rewording surveys for second-language speakers and adding translations of the questions to solve data missing at random or through a redesign of data collection methods, such as observing sensitive information rather than asking for this information directly from participants, to find nonignorable missing values.

A rough understanding of why certain data is missing can also help to influence how you manage and treat missing values. If male participants, for example, are more willing to supply information about their salary than female participants, this would eliminate using the mean (of mostly male respondents) from the existing data to populate the missing values (of mostly female respondents).

Managing MCAR is relatively straightforward as the data values collected can be considered a random sample and are more easily aggregated or estimated. We'll discuss common methods for filling missing values in this chapter, but first, let's review the code in Python for inspecting missing values.

```
df.isnull().sum()
```

```
1  import pandas as pd
2
3  df = pd.read_csv('~/Downloads/listings.csv')
4
5  df.isnull().sum()
6
```

```
id                                  0
name                               59
host_id                             0
host_name                          26
neighbourhood_group                 0
neighbourhood                       0
latitude                            0
longitude                           0
room_type                           0
price                               0
minimum_nights                      0
number_of_reviews                   0
last_review                      3908
reviews_per_month                3914
calculated_host_listings_count      0
availability_365                    0
dtype: int64
```

Figure 18: Inspecting missing values using isnull().sum()

Using this method, we can obtain a general overview of missing values for each feature. From here, we can see that four variables contain missing values, which is high in the case of **last_review** (3908) and **reviews_per_month** (3914). While this won't be necessary for use with all algorithms, there are several options we can consider to fill these missing values. The first approach is to fill the missing values with the average value for that variable using the `fill.na` method.

```
df['reviews_per_month'].fillna((df['reviews_per_month'].mean()),inpla
ce=True)
```

This line of code replaces the missing values for the variable `reviews_per_month` with the mean (average) value of that variable, which is 1.135525 for this variable.

Note that the mean method does not apply to non-numeric data such as strings—as these values can't be aggregated to the mean.

One-hot encoded variables and Boolean variables expressed as 0 or 1 should also not be filled using the mean method. For variables expressed as 0 or 1, it's not possible to aggregate these values to say 0.5 or 0.75 as this changes the meaning of the variable.

Another way of using the `fill.na` method is to approximate missing values with the mode (the most common value in the dataset for that variable).

```
df['reviews_per_month'].fillna(df['reviews_per_month'].mode(),inplace=True)
```

In the case of our dataset, the mode value for this variable is 'NAN' (Not a Number), and there isn't a reliable mode value we can use. This is common when variable values are expressed as a floating-point number rather than an integer (whole number).

To fill in missing values with a customized value, such as '0', we can specify that target value inside the parentheses.

```
df['reviews_per_month'].fillna(0)
```

A more drastic measure is to drop rows or columns with large amounts of missing values from the analysis. Removing missing values becomes necessary when neither the mean and mode or finding an artificial value are reliable stop-gap solutions. Removing values is also recommended when missing values are confined to a small percentage of data points or for removing a variable that's not central to your analysis.[12]

There are two primary methods for removing missing values. The first is to manually remove entire columns with missing values using the `del` function as demonstrated earlier. The second method is the `dropna` method (demonstrated below) which

---

[12] Sarah Boslaugh, "Statistics in a Nutshell," *O'Reilly Media*, Second Edition, 2012.

automatically removes columns or rows that contain missing values on a case-by-case basis.

```
df.dropna(axis = 0, how = 'any', subset = None, inplace = True)
```

As datasets typically have more rows than columns, it's usually best to drop rows rather than columns as this helps to retain more of the original data. A detailed explanation of the parameters for this technique is included in Table 5.

Parameter	Argument	Explanation	Default
axis	0	Drops rows with missing values	✓
	1	Drops columns with missing values	
how	any	Drops rows or columns with any missing values	✓
	all	Drops rows or columns with all values missing	
subset	variable	Define which columns to search for missing values, i.e. 'genre'	
	None	Select "None" if you do not wish to set a subset.	
inplace	True	If True, do operation inplace (update rather than replace)	
	False		✓

Table 5: Dropna parameters

In summary, there isn't always a simple solution for dealing with missing values and your response will often depend on the data type and the frequency of the missing values. In the case of the Berlin Airbnb dataset, there is a high number of missing values for the variables **last_review** and **reviews_per_month**, which warrants removing these variables. Alternatively, we could use the mean to fill **reviews_per_month** given these values are expressed numerically and can be easily aggregated. The other variable **last_review** cannot be aggregated because it's expressed as a timestamp rather than as an integer or floating-point number.

The other variables containing missing values, **name** and **host_name**, are also problematic and cannot be filled with artificial values. Given these two variables are discrete variables, they cannot be estimated using the mean and mode, and should perhaps be removed on a row-by-row basis given the low number of missing values for these two variables.

Documentation for Dropna: http://bit.ly/2KqV1a7

Dimension Reduction

Dimension reduction, known also as *descending dimension algorithms*, is a method of transforming data to a lower dimension, which can help to lessen computational resources and visualize patterns in the data.

Dimensions are the number of variables describing the data, such as the city of residence, country of residence, age, and sex of a user. Up to four variables can be plotted on a scatterplot but three-dimensional and two-dimensional plots are easiest for human eyes to interpret.

The goal of descending dimension algorithms is to arrive at a minimal set of variables that mimic the distribution of the original dataset's variables. Reducing the number of variables makes it easier to recognize patterns, including natural groupings as well as outliers and anomalies.

It's important to note that dimension reduction isn't a case of deleting columns but, rather, mathematically transforming information contained in those columns in such a way that the information is captured using fewer variables (columns). If, for example, we look at house prices, we might find multiple correlated variables (such as house area and postcode) that we can merge into a new variable that adequately represents those two variables. By applying dimension reduction before running the core algorithm, the model will run faster, consume less computational resources, and may actually provide more accurate predictions.

Another side benefit of this technique is the opportunity to visualize multi-dimensional data. Given the maximum number of plottable dimensions for a scatterplot is four, and two or three dimensions is ideal (the fourth dimension is time[13]), descending dimension algorithms can be used to streamline a dataset with more than four dimensions into four or fewer variables and project the synthetic variables onto the visual workspace of a scatterplot.

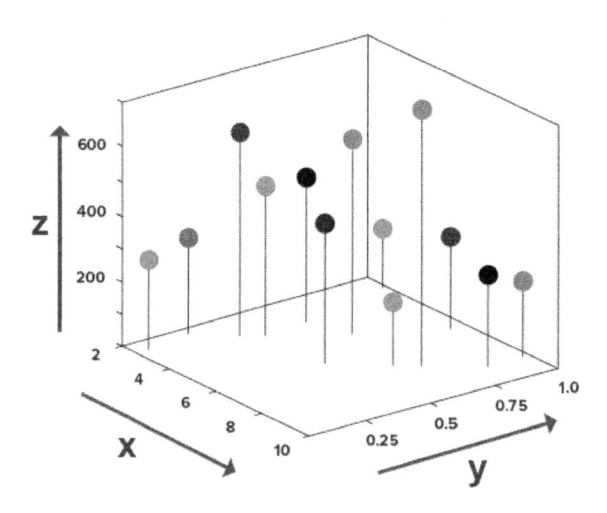

Figure 19: Three-dimensional scatterplot with three variables

The ability to visualize relationships and patterns on a scatterplot is useful for both explanatory and exploratory graphics. Exploratory graphics are typically generated on the fly to aid internal understanding when the analysis is in progress, whereas explanatory graphics are delivered to an external audience in the post-analysis stage.

---

[13] A 4-D plot is essentially a dynamic/moving 3-D plot, such as visualizing a patient's internal anatomy moving in real-time.

Bear in mind, though, that streamlining a multidimensional dataset into four or fewer variables (suitable for a scatterplot) isn't a prerequisite for machine learning. Models that analyze the input of 20 variables, for instance, can't be visualized on a scatterplot but can still be processed by the model to identify patterns and aid decision-making by producing a binary output such as 1 (True) and 0 (False) or another form of output.

QUIZ

1) Which method can we use to view the bottom *n* rows of a Pandas dataframe?

a. head()
b. tail()
c. describe()
d. columns

2) Which method can we use to view the top *n* rows of a Pandas dataframe?

a. head()
b. tail()
c. describe()
d. columns

3) Which method can we use to generate a summary of the dataframe's mean, standard deviation, and IQR values?

a. head()
b. tail()
c. describe()
d. columns

4) Which technique is not an example of exploratory data visualization?

a. heatmap
b. pairplot
c. shape
d. scatterplot

5) Which code command can we use to preview a Pandas dataframe (df) inside a notebook?

a. df.head()
b. df_head()
c. df.header()
d. df.shape()

SOLUTIONS

1) b, tail()

2) a, head()

3) c, describe()

4) c, shape

5) a, df.head()

6

PRE-MODEL ALGORITHMS

As an extension of the data scrubbing process, unsupervised learning algorithms are sometimes used in advance of a supervised learning algorithm to prepare the data for prediction modeling. In this way, unsupervised algorithms are used to clean or reshape the data rather than to derive actionable insight.

Examples of pre-model algorithms include dimension reduction techniques, as introduced in the previous chapter, as well as *k-means clustering*. Both of these algorithms are examined in this chapter.

Principal Component Analysis

One of the most popular dimension reduction techniques is principal component analysis (PCA). Known also as *general factor analysis*, PCA is useful for dramatically reducing data complexity and visualizing data in fewer dimensions. The practical goal of PCA is to find a low-dimensional representation of the dataset that preserves as much of the original variation as possible. Rather than removing individual features from the dataset, PCA recreates dimensions as a linear combination of features called *components* and then ranks components that contribute most to patterns in the data, allowing you to drop components that have the least impact on data variability.

In practice, the initial aim of PCA is to place the first axis in the direction of the greatest variance of the data points and maximize the variance depicted along that axis. A second axis is then placed perpendicular (on a 90-degree angle) to the first axis to form an orthogonal line, which creates the first two components. In a two-dimensional setting, the location of the second axis is fixed according to the position of the first axis. In a three-dimensional space, where there are more options to place the second axis perpendicular to the first axis, the aim is to position it in a way that maximizes the variance on its axis.

An example of PCA in a two-dimensional space is demonstrated in Figure 20.

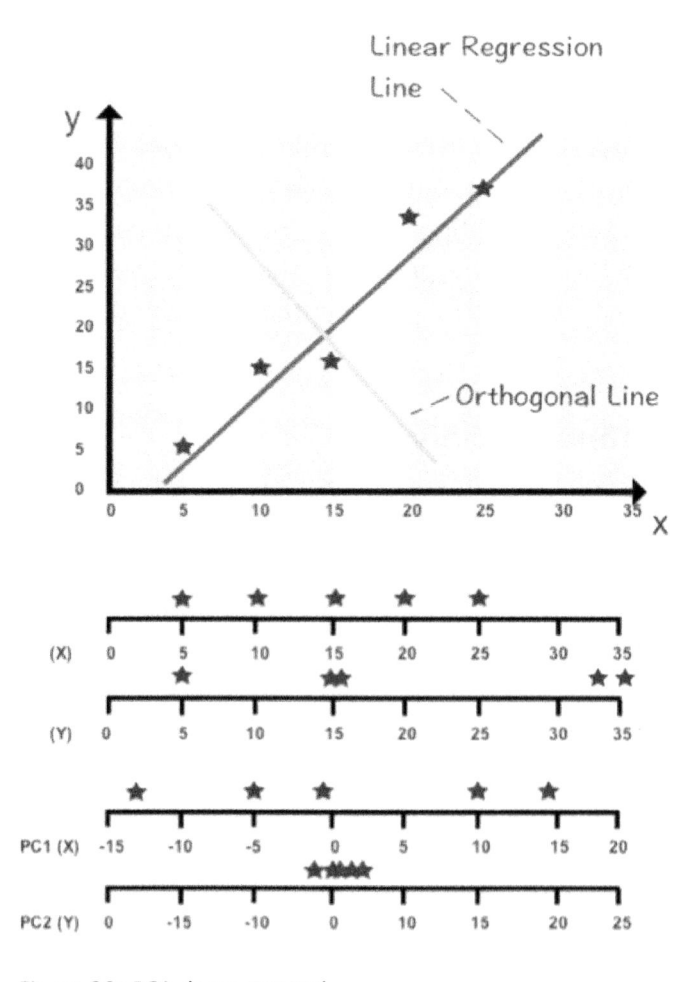

Figure 20: PCA deconstructed

Above are four horizontal axes. The first two axes measure the x and y values from the original data. The second two axes measure the distance from the x and y values when rotated 90 degrees. To visualize the rotated axes, the orthogonal line can be used as an artificial y-axis and the linear regression line assumes the role of the x-axis as shown in Figure 20.

These new axes provide us with the first two components for this dataset. The new x-axis is principal component 1 (PC 1) and the new y-axis is principal component 2 (PC 2). Using PC1 and PC2 values (depicted on the third and fourth axis), we can see a new range of variance among the data points. The variance in PC1 has expanded in comparison to the original x values (seen on the first axis). Meanwhile, the variance in PC2 has shrunk significantly as all the data points are close to zero and virtually stacked on top of each other.

Given that PC2 contributes the least to overall variance, we can focus our attention on studying the variance contained in PC1. While PC1 doesn't contain 100% of the original information, it captures the variable relationship that has the most impact on data patterns while minimizing computational resources.

In this example, we divided the dataset into two components before selecting one principal component. In other scenarios, you might select two or three principal components containing 75% of the original data from a total of ten components. Of course, insisting on 100% of the information would defeat the purpose of data reduction and maximizing performance. In addition, there is no well-accepted method for determining an appropriate number of principal components to achieve an optimal representation of the data. Selecting the number of components to analyze is a subjective decision that is judged by the size of the dataset and to what extent you wish to shrink the data.

Exercise 1

In this first code exercise, we will reduce a dataset to its two principal components. The dataset used for this exercise is the

Advertising Dataset, which is available for download at http://scatterplotpress.com/p/datasets.

Feature	Data Type	Continuous/Discrete
Daily Time Spent on Site	Floating-point	Continuous
Age	Integer	Continuous
Area Income	Floating-point	Continuous
Daily Internet Usage	Floating-point	Continuous
Ad Topic Line	String	Discrete
City	String	Discrete
Male	Boolean	Discrete
Country	String	Discrete
Timestamp	TimeDate	Discrete
Clicked on Ad	Boolean	Discrete

Table 6: Advertising dataset

1) Import libraries

Let's begin by importing the following Python libraries: NumPy, Pandas, Seaborn, Matplotlib Pyplot, and Matplotlib inline. Each of these libraries can be imported by entering the following code inside a new Jupyter notebook.

```
import numpy as np
import pandas as pd
import seaborn as sns
import matplotlib.pyplot as plt
%matplotlib inline
```

2) Import dataset

The second step is to import the dataset into the same cell. After logging on to kaggle.com, you can download the Advertising Dataset as a zip file. Next, unzip the downloaded file and import the CSV file into Jupyter Notebook using `pd.read_csv()` and adding the file directory according to your operating system.

```
df = pd.read_csv('~/Downloads/advertising.csv')
```

This loads the dataset into a Pandas dataframe. You can review the dataframe using the `head()` command and clicking "Run" or by navigating to Cell > Run All from the top menu.

```
df.head()
```

```
In [2]: import numpy as np
        import pandas as pd
        import seaborn as sns
        import matplotlib.pyplot as plt
        %matplotlib inline

        df = pd.read_csv('~/Downloads/advertising.csv')
        df.head()
```

	Daily Time Spent on Site	Age	Area Income	Daily Internet Usage	Ad Topic Line	City	Male	Country	Timestamp	Clicked on Ad
0	68.95	35	61833.90	256.09	Cloned 5thgeneration orchestration	Wrightburgh	0	Tunisia	2016-03-27 00:53:11	0
1	80.23	31	68441.85	193.77	Monitored national standardization	West Jodi	1	Nauru	2016-04-04 01:39:02	0
2	69.47	26	59785.94	236.50	Organic bottom-line service-desk	Davidton	0	San Marino	2016-03-13 20:35:42	0
3	74.15	29	54806.18	245.89	Triple-buffered reciprocal time-frame	West Terrifurt	1	Italy	2016-01-10 02:31:19	0
4	68.37	35	73889.99	225.58	Robust logistical utilization	South Manuel	0	Iceland	2016-06-03 03:36:18	0

We can see that the dataset comprises 10 features including **Daily Time Spent on Site, Age, Area Income, Daily Internet Usage, Ad Topic Line, City, Male, Country, Timestamp,** and **Clicked on Ad**.

3) Remove features

Next, we need to remove non-numerical features that can't be parsed by this algorithm, which includes **Ad Topic Line, City, Country,** and **Timestamp**. Although the **Timestamp** values are expressed in numerals, their special formatting is not compatible with the mathematical calculations that must be made between variables using this algorithm.

We also need to remove the discrete variable **Male**, which is expressed as an integer (0 or 1), as our model only examines continuous input features.[14]

Let's remove the five features from the dataset using the `del` function and specifying the column titles we wish to remove.

```
del df['Ad Topic Line']
del df['City']
del df['Country']
del df['Timestamp']
del df['Male']
```

4) Scale data

Next we will import the Scikit-learn function `StandardScaler`, which will be used to standardize features by using zero as the mean for all variables and scaling to unit variance. The mean and standard deviation are then stored and used later with the transform method (recreates the dataframe with the requested transformed values).

```
#Import StandardScaler
from sklearn.preprocessing import StandardScaler
```

After importing StandardScaler, we can assign it as a new variable, `fit` the function to the features contained in the dataframe, and `transform` those values under a new variable name.

```
scaler = StandardScaler()
scaler.fit(df)
scaled_data = scaler.transform(df)
```

---

[14] PCA is commonly used with continuous variables and also in preparation for use with supervised algorithms that run only with continuous variables. There are more appropriate techniques to handle a mix of continuous and discrete variable types including Multiple Factor Analysis.

StandardScaler is often used in conjunction with PCA and other algorithms including *k*-nearest neighbors and support vector machines to rescale and standardize data features. This gives the dataset the properties of a standard normal distribution with a mean of zero and a standard deviation of one.

Without standardization, the PCA algorithm is likely to lock onto features that maximize variance but that could be exaggerated by another factor. To provide an example, the variance of **Age** changes dramatically when measured in days in place of years, and if left unchecked, this type of formatting might mislead the selection of components which is based on maximizing variance. StandardScaler helps to avoid this problem by rescaling and standardizing variables.

Conversely, standardization might not be necessary for PCA if the scale of the variables is relevant to your analysis or consistent across variables.

Further information regarding StandardScaler can be found at https://scikit-learn.org/stable/modules/generated/sklearn.preprocessing.StandardScaler.html.

5) Assign algorithm

Having laid much of the groundwork for our model, we can now import the PCA algorithm from Scikit-learn's decomposition library.

```
from sklearn.decomposition import PCA
```

Take careful note of the next line of code as this is where we reshape the dataframe's features into a defined number of components. For this exercise, we want to find the components that have the most impact on data variability. By setting the number of components to 2 (`n_components=2`), we're asking PCA to find the two components that best explain variability in the data. The number of components can be modified according to your requirements, but two components is the simplest to interpret and visualize on a scatterplot.

```
pca = PCA(n_components=2)
```

Next, we need to `fit` the two components to our scaled data and recreate the dataframe's values using the `transform` method.

```
pca.fit(scaled_data)
scaled_pca = pca.transform(scaled_data)
```

Let's check the transformation using the `shape` command to compare the two datasets.

```
#Query the number of rows and columns in the scaled dataframe
scaled_data.shape
```

Output: (1000, 5)

Now query the shape of the scaled PCA dataframe.

```
#Query the number of rows and columns in the scaled PCA dataframe
scaled_pca.shape
```

Output: (1000, 2)

We can see that the scaled dataframe has been compressed from 1,000 rows with 5 columns to 1,000 rows with 2 columns using PCA.

6) Visualize the output

Let's use the Python plotting library Matplotlib to visualize the two principal components on a 2-D scatterplot, with principal component 1 marked on the x-axis and principal component 2 on the y-axis.

We'll visualize the two principal components without a color legend in the first version of the code before adding code for the color legend in the second version.

Version 1: Visualized plot

```
#State the size of the plot
plt.figure(figsize=(10,8))


#Configure the scatterplot's x and y axes as principal components 1
and 2, and color-coded by the variable Clicked on Ad.
plt.scatter(scaled_pca[:, 0],scaled_pca[:, 1],c=df['Clicked on Ad'])


#State the scatterplot labels
plt.xlabel('First Principal Component')
plt.ylabel('Second Principal Component')
```

Click Run to generate the plot in Jupyter Notebook.

[Scatter plot: First Principal Component (x-axis) vs Second Principal Component (y-axis)]

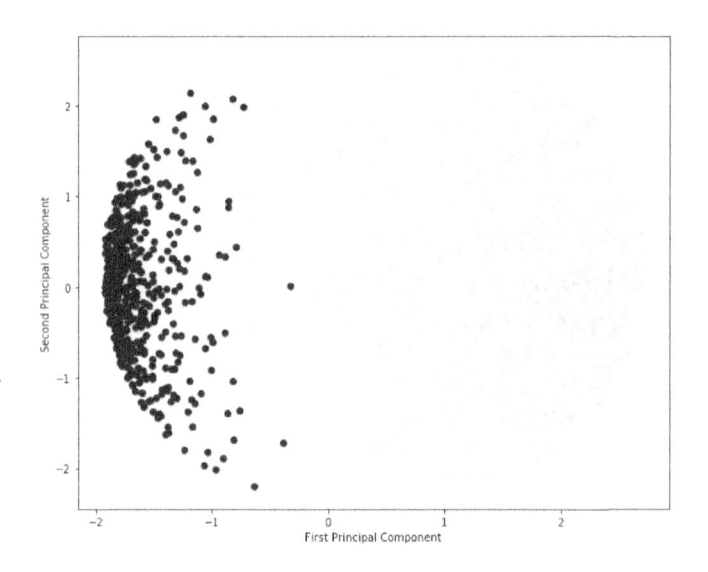

The two components are color-coded to delineate the outcome of Clicked on Ad (Clicked/Did not click). Keep in mind that components don't correspond to a single variable but rather a combination of variables.

Finally, we can modify the code to add a color legend. This is a more advanced set of code and requires the use of a for-loop in Python and RGB color codes that can be found at Rapidtables.com.

Version 2: Visualized plot with color legend

```
plt.figure(figsize=(10,8))
legend = df['Clicked on Ad']

#Add indigo and yellow RGB colors
colors = {0: '#4B0082', 1: '#FFFF00'}
labels = {0: 'Clicked', 1: 'Did not click'}

#Use a for-loop to set color for each data point
```

```
for t in np.unique(legend):
    ix = np.where(legend == t)
    plt.scatter(scaled_pca[ix,0], scaled_pca[ix,1], c=colors[t],
label=labels[t])


plt.xlabel('First Principal Component')
plt.ylabel('Second Principal Component')
plt.legend()
plt.show()
```

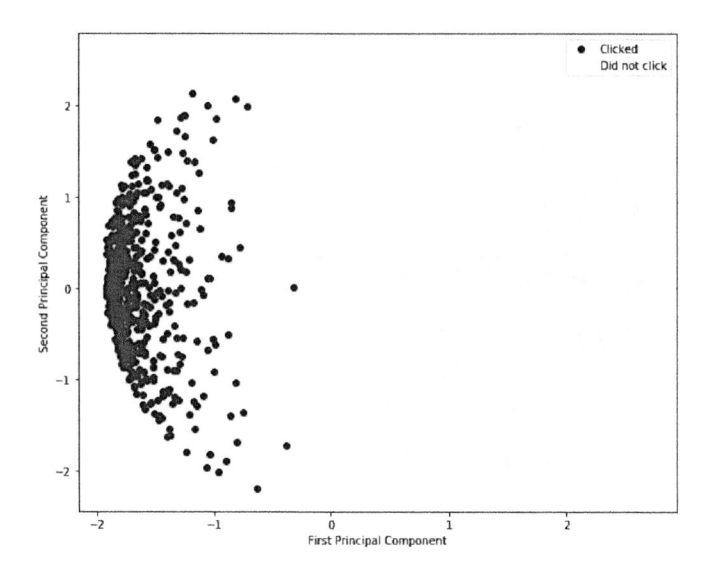

From this visualization, we can see the clear separation of outcomes with the aid of a color legend in the top right corner. The output of PCA is now ready for further analysis using a supervised learning technique such as logistic regression or *k*-nearest neighbors.

Documentation for PCA: http://bit.ly/31ythG2

k-Means Clustering

Another popular technique to reduce data complexity is *k*-means clustering, which is used for identifying groups of data points without prior knowledge of existing classes.

Original Data   Clustered Data

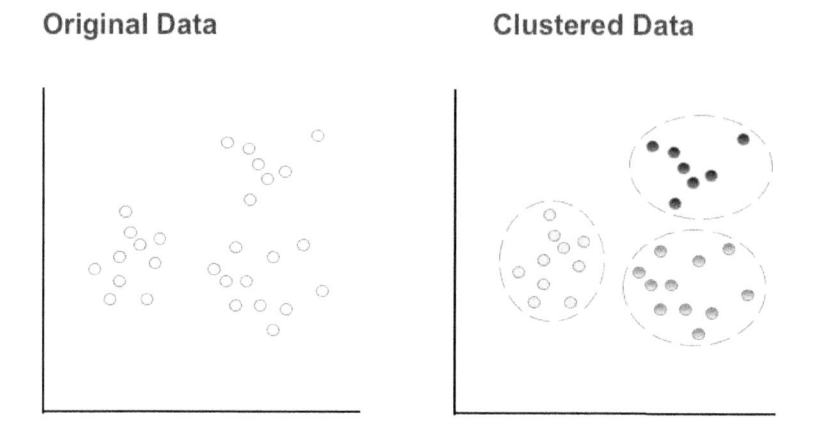

Figure 21: Comparison of original data and clustered data using *k*-means clustering

K-means clustering splits the dataset into *k* number of clusters, with *k* representing the number of clusters. Setting *k* to "3," for example, splits the data into three clusters.

Each cluster is assigned a random centroid, which is a data point that becomes the epicenter of an individual cluster. The remaining data points are assigned to the closest centroid. The centroid coordinates are then updated based on the mean of the new cluster. This update may cause some data points to switch allegiance and join a new cluster based on comparative proximity with a different centroid. If so, the centroid coordinates are recalculated and updated. The algorithm reaches completion when all data points remain in the same cluster following an update in centroid coordinates, which will produce the final set of clusters.

Exercise 2

In this second exercise we will generate an artificial dataset and use *k*-means clustering to split the data into four natural groupings.

1) Import libraries

The artificial dataset used for this exercise is generated using `make_blobs` from Scikit-learn and grouped using the *k*-means algorithm. Visualization will be required for this exercise using Matplotlib Pyplot and Matplotlib inline.

```
import numpy as np
from sklearn.datasets import make_blobs
from sklearn.cluster import KMeans
import matplotlib.pyplot as plt
%matplotlib inline
```

2) Create blobs

Rather than import a dataset for this exercise, we are using `make_blobs` to generate an artificial dataset with 300 samples, 2 features, and 4 centers with a cluster standard deviation of 4.

```
X, y = make_blobs(n_samples=300, n_features=2, centers=4,
cluster_std=4, random_state=10)
```

Let's now plot the artificial dataset using a scatterplot from Matplotlib Pyplot.

```
plt.figure(figsize=(7,5))
plt.scatter(X[:, 0], X[:, 1])
```

Run the model in Jupyter Notebook to generate the following scatterplot.

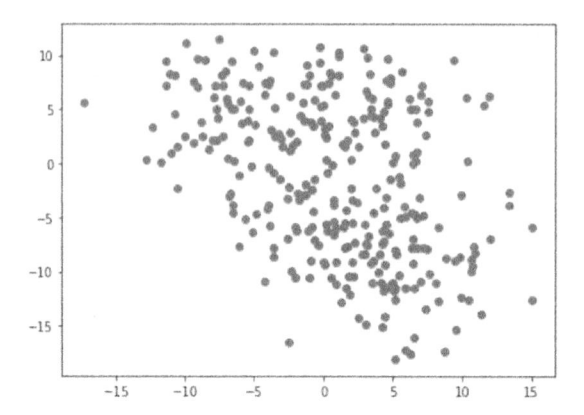

3) Set algorithm

We now want to use *k*-means clustering to discover natural groupings among data points that share similar attributes. By establishing a new variable (**model**), we can call the KMeans algorithm from Scikit-learn and assign the initial number of clusters to 4, before fitting the model to the artificial data (X).

```
model = KMeans(n_clusters=4)
model.fit(X)
```

4) Predict

Using the `predict` function under a new variable (`model_predict`), we can execute the model and generate the centroid coordinates using `cluster_centers_`.

```
model_predict = model.predict(X)
centroids = model.cluster_centers_
print(model.cluster_centers_)
```

Run the model in Jupyter Notebook to print the x and y coordinates of the model's cluster centers (centroids).

```
[[ 3.23209343  4.94623366]
 [ 6.24946744 -9.70847466]
 [-1.01492539 -5.23271226]
 [-7.03502629  4.80055552]]
```

This prints the four centroid positions, which we will use in Step 5.

5) Visualize the output

It's now time to plot the clusters on a scatterplot using two sets of elements. The first is the four color-coded clusters produced using the *k*-means model stored under the variable named **model_predict**. The second is the cluster centroids, stored under the variable named **centroids**.

The centroids are represented in black with a marker size (s) of 200 and an alpha of 1. Alpha can take any float number between 0 and 1.0, with 0 equal to maximum transparency and 1 equal to opaque. As we are superimposing the four cluster centroids over the four clusters, we need the alpha to be 1 (opaque).

More information about Matplotlib scatterplot features can be found at
https://matplotlib.org/3.1.1/api/_as_gen/matplotlib.pyplot.scatter.html.

```
plt.figure(figsize=(7,5))
plt.scatter(X[:, 0], X[:, 1], c=model_predict, s=50, cmap='rainbow')
plt.scatter(centroids[:, 0], centroids[:, 1], c='black', s=200,
alpha=1);
```

Run the model in Jupyter Notebook to produce the following scatterplot with the four clusters and their corresponding centroids superimposed in front.

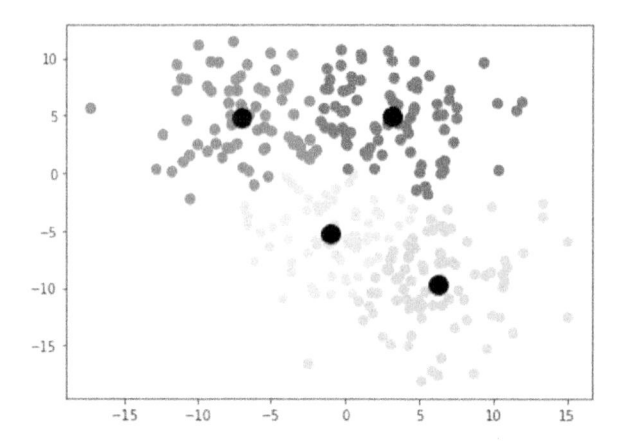

As a result of *k*-means clustering, we have identified four previously unknown groupings within our dataset and streamlined 300 data points into four centroids that we can use to generalize the data.

As mentioned in the previous chapter, *k*-means clustering is useful for reducing a dataset with a very high number of rows/data points into a more manageable number of cluster centroids before feeding that data into a supervised learning algorithm. Alternatively, you may wish to further analyze the data points contained in individual clusters using supervised learning or another unsupervised learning technique. You may even wish to apply *k*-means clustering to one of the identified clusters, which is useful in the case of market research such as identifying subsets of customers.

Scree plot

To optimize *k*, you may wish to analyze a scree plot for guidance. A scree plot visualizes the degree of scattering (variance) by comparing the distortion for each variation of clusters. Distortion is measured (usually using Euclidean distance) as the average of the squared distance between the centroid and the other data points in that cluster.

To determine the optimal number of clusters, we have to select the value of *k* where distortion subsides dramatically to the left of the scree plot but before it reaches a point of negligible change with cluster variations to the right. This means that from the optimal data point (the "elbow" point), distortion should start decreasing linearly to the right.

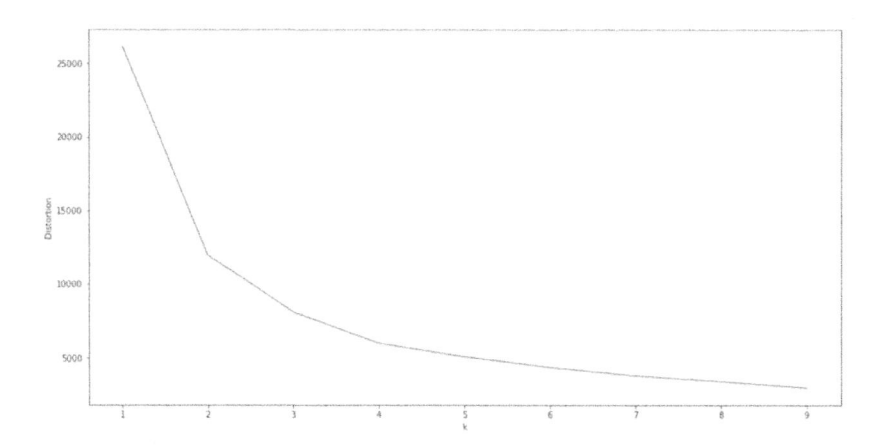

In the case of our model, the optimal number appears to be 3 or 4 clusters—as there exists a significant kink to the left of these two cluster combinations due to a pronounced drop-off in distortion. Meanwhile, there is also a linear decline to the right, especially for *k*=4. This also makes sense given that the dataset was artificially generated with **centers** set to 4.

Using Python, we can code the scree plot above by iterating the values of *k* from 1 to 10 and calculating the values of distortion for each *k* value. This involves using the for loop function in Python and then using Matplotlib to plot the scree plot as shown below.

```
#Using a for loop, iterate the values of k with a range of 1-10 and
find the values of distortion for each k value.
```

```
distortions = []
K = range(1,10)
for k in K:
    model = KMeans(n_clusters=k)
    model.fit(X, y)
    distortions.append(model.inertia_)

#Generate plot with k on the x-axis and distortions on the y_axis using matplotlib
plt.figure(figsize=(16,8))
plt.plot(K, distortions)
plt.xlabel('k')
plt.ylabel('Distortion')
plt.show()
```

Documentation for k-means Clustering: http://bit.ly/2Z2IDkQ

QUIZ

1) Which solution will best shrink and simplify the original dataset?

a. pca = PCA(n_components=10)
b. pca = PCA(n_components=12)
c. pca = PCA(n_components=3)
d. pca = PCA(n_components=max)

2) StandardScaler is often used in conjunction with PCA and which other algorithm to rescale and standardize features?

a. Support vector machines
b. Linear regression
c. Multiple linear regression
d. Support vector machines

3) For k-means clustering, which technique might we use to find the appropriate number of clusters?

a. Big elbow method
b. Mean absolute error
c. Scree plot
d. One-hot encoding

4) Using k-means clustering, the total number of centroids should be lower than the total number of variables in the original dataset. True or False?

5) In Python, you can use _____ to code a scree plot.

a. object-orientated programming

b. polymorphism
c. the Elbow method
d. a for loop

SOLUTIONS

1) c, pca = PCA(n_components=3)

2) a, Support vector machines

3) c, Scree plot

4) True

5) d, a for loop

SPLIT VALIDATION

A crucial part of machine learning is partitioning the data into two separate sets using a technique called *split validation*. The first set is called the *training data* and is used to build the prediction model. The second set is called the test data and is kept in reserve and used to assess the accuracy of the model developed from the training data. The training and test data is typically split 70/30 or 80/20 with the training data representing the larger portion. Once the model has been optimized and validated against the test data for accuracy, it's ready to generate predictions using new input data.

Although the model is used on both the training and test sets, it's from the training data alone that the model is built. The test data is used as input to form predictions and assess the model's accuracy, but it is never decoded and should not be used to create the model. As the test data cannot be used to build and optimize the model, data scientists sometimes use a third independent dataset called the *validation set*. After building an initial model with the training set, the validation set can be fed to the prediction model and used as feedback to optimize the model's hyperparameters. The test set is then used to assess the prediction error of the final model.

To maximize data utility, it is possible to reuse the validation and test data as training data. This would involve bundling the used data with the original training data to optimize the model just before it's put into use. However, once the original validation or test set has been used for training, it can no longer be used as a validation or test set.

To perform split validation in Python we can use `train_test_split` from Scikit-learn, which requires an initial import from the `sklearn.model_selection` library.

```
from sklearn.model_selection import train_test_split
```

Before using this code library, we first need to set our X and y values.

```
import pandas as pd
df = pd.read_csv('~/Downloads/advertising.csv')
X = df[['Daily Time Spent on Site', 'Age', 'Area Income', 'Daily Internet Usage', 'Ad Topic Line', 'Country']]
y = df['Clicked on Ad']
```

We are now ready to create our training and test data using the following parameters: `train_size` (optional), `test_size`, `random_state` (optional), and `shuffle` (optional).

Parameter	Argument	Explanation	Default
test_size	Float (between 0 and 1.0)	Proportion of test size, i.e. 0.3 = 30%	0.25 (if train_size is not specified)
	Integer	The number of test samples, i.e. 40 = for 40 test samples	
	None	Test value is automatically set to complement that of train_size.	
train_size (optional)	Float (between 0 and 1.0)	Proportion of test size, i.e. 0.7 = 70%	
	Integer	Number of test samples, i.e. 60 = for 60 test samples	
random_state (optional)	Integer	A seed number (integer) that can be reused to replicate the same random split. This ensures the model uses the same data split each time it's used.	
	None	A random seed number is used.	None
Shuffle (optional)	True	Data is shuffled	True
	False	Data is not shuffled	

Table 7: Split validation parameters

```
X_train, X_test, y_train, y_test = train_test_split(X, y,
test_size=0.3, random_state=10, shuffle=True)
```

In this example, the training/test data is split 70/30 and shuffled, with a random seed of 10 'bookmarked' for future code replication.

Train Test Split Documentation: http://bit.ly/2KqPv7s

Validation Set

At the time of writing, Scikit-learn does not provide a specific function to create a three-way train/validation/test split. However, one quick solution is to split the test data into two partitions as demonstrated below.

```
X_train, X_test, y_train, y_test = train_test_split(X, y,
test_size=0.4)
```

This sets the training data to 60% and the test data to 40%. The test data is then split 50/50 so that the test data and validation set are each equivalent to 20% of the original data.

```
X_test, X_val, y_test, y_val = train_test_split(X_test, y_test,
test_size=0.5)
```

QUIZ

1) Which code argument can we use to replicate the same random spit of the same data?

a. shuffle
b. random_state
c. train_size
d. test_size

2) The following code is an example of which technique?

X_test, X_val, y_test, y_val = train_test_split(X_test, y_test, test_size=0.7)

a. Split validation
b. Cross validation
c. Bucketing
d. Exploratory data analysis

3) Which argument should we use to set the training data to 60% of the original dataset as part of split validation?

a. test_size =0.4
b. training_size = 0.6
c. test_size=0.6
d. random_state=True

4) Which library should we use to perform split validation?

a. Pandas
b. Scikit-learn
c. Seaborn
d. NumPy

5) The training set is usually smaller than the test set to ensure higher prediction accuracy. True or False?

SOLUTIONS

1) b, random_state

2) a, Split validation

3) a, test_size = 0.4

4) b, Scikit-learn

5) False (More data is required in training to build the model)

8

MODEL DESIGN

Before we explore specific supervised learning algorithms, it's useful to pause and take a high-level look at the full procedure of building a machine learning model. This involves reviewing a number of steps examined in the preceding chapters as well as new methods including *evaluate* and *predict*. These 10 steps take place inside your development environment and follow a relatively fixed sequence. Once you are familiar with this framework, you will find it easy to design your own machine learning models from start to finish.

IMPORT LIBRARIES
IMPORT DATASET
EDA
DATA SCRUBBING
PRE-MODEL ALGORITHM
SPLIT VALIDATION
SET ALGORITHM
PREDICT
EVALUATE
OPTIMIZE

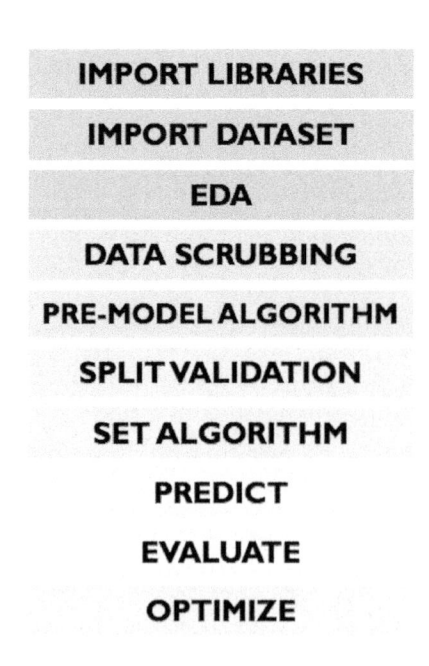

Figure 22: An overview of designing a machine learning model

1) Import libraries

Given the Python interpreter works from top to bottom through your code, it's vital to import libraries before calling any of their specific functions. If you attempt to create a heatmap or pairplot without first importing Seaborn and Matplolib, the Python interpreter won't be able to process your request.

The libraries don't necessarily need to be placed in the top section of your notebook. Some data scientists, for instance, prefer to import specific algorithm-based libraries in sections where they are used—as long as the import is made ahead of code references to that library.

2) Import dataset

Datasets are generally imported from your organization's records or public repositories such as Kaggle.com. While Kaggle.com has a fantastic offering of datasets, it's worth mentioning that Scikit-learn offers a number of small built-in datasets that don't necessitate an external download. As noted by Scikit-learn, these datasets are useful for beginners to gain a feel for new algorithms. Scikit-learn's datasets are summarized below and can be imported directly into your notebook.

Dataset Name	Code	Suggested Use Case
Boston House-Prices Dataset	load_boston	Regression
Iris Dataset	load_iris	Classification
Diabetes Dataset	load_diabetes	Regression
Digits Dataset	load_digits	Classification
Linnerud Dataset	load_linnerud	Multivariate regression
Wine Dataset	load_wine	Classification
Breast Cancer Wisconsin Dataset	load_breast_cancer	Classification

Table 8: Built-in datasets available with Scikit-learn, http://scikit-learn.org/stable/datasets/index.html

Code example:

```
from sklearn.datasets import load_breast_cancer
```

```
cancer = load_breast_cancer()
```

Make Blobs

Using Scikit-learn, you can self-generate a random dataset using a function called make blobs, as used in Chapter 6 with *k*-means clustering. Again, this data is useful for gaining confidence with a new algorithm rather than unearthing meaningful insight.

Code example:
```
from sklearn.datasets import make_blobs
data = make_blobs(n_samples=200, n_features=2, centers=4,
cluster_std=1.8, random_state=101)
```

Parameter	Explanation	Default
n_samples	If integer, the number of cases are divided among clusters	100
n_features	The number of features	2
centers	The number of centers to generate	NA
cluster_std	Float, the standard deviation of the clusters	1.0
random_state	Determines random number generation for dataset creation and reproducible output	NA

Table 9: Parameters for making blobs

Documentation for Make Blobs: http://bit.ly/2GYV0Ir

3) Exploratory data analysis

The third step, exploratory data analysis (EDA), provides an opportunity to get familiar with your data including distribution and the state of missing values. Exploratory data analysis also drives the next stage of data scrubbing and your choice of algorithm.

In addition, EDA may come into play in other sections of your code as you check the size and structure of your dataset and integrate that feedback to direct model optimization.

4) Data scrubbing

The data scrubbing stage, as detailed in Chapter 5, usually consumes the most time and effort in developing a prediction model. Like looking after a good pair of dress shoes, it's important to pay attention to the quality and composition of your data. This means cleaning up the data, inspecting its value, making repairs, and also knowing when to throw it out.

5) Pre-model algorithm (optional)

As an optional extension of the data scrubbing process, unsupervised learning techniques including *k*-means clustering analysis and descending dimension algorithms are sometimes used in preparation for analyzing large and complex datasets. The technique *k*-means clustering, as explored in Chapter 6, can be used to reduce row volume by compressing rows into a lower number of clusters based on similar values, before conducting further analysis using supervised learning.

This step, though, is optional and does not apply to every model, particularly for small datasets with a low number of dimensions (features) or rows.

6) Split validation

As described in Chapter 7, split validation is used to partition the data for the purpose of training and test analysis. It's also useful to randomize your data at this point using the shuffle feature and to set a random state if you want to replicate the model's output in the future.

7) Set algorithm

Algorithms are the headline act for every machine learning model and must be chosen carefully. The algorithm itself is a mathematical-based sequence of steps that reacts to changing patterns to generate a decision or output. By executing a series of steps defined by the algorithm, the model reacts to input variables to interpret patterns, make calculations, and reach decisions.

As input data is variable, algorithms can produce different outputs based on the input data. Algorithms are also malleable in that they have hyperparameters which can be adjusted to create a more customized model. Algorithms are, thus, a moving framework rather than a concrete equation and are customizable based on the target output and the characteristics of the input data.

For context, the algorithm should not be confused or mistaken for the model. The model is the final state of the algorithm (after hyperparameters are consolidated in response to patterns learned from the data) and the combination of data scrubbing, split validation, and evaluation techniques.

Below is a list of popular algorithms used in machine learning and their common characteristics.

Algorithm	Target Output	Data	Methodology	Computing Resources	Potential Accuracy	Transparency
Linear Regression	Continuous	Linear patterns, no missing values, limited volume	Supervised	Low	Medium	High
Logistic Regression	Discrete	Reliable patterns, limited volume, limited outliers	Supervised	Low	Medium	Medium
k-means	Discrete	Complex data	Unsupervised	Medium	Medium	High
k-NN	Discrete	No missing values, limited dimensions	Supervised	Medium	Medium	High
Decision Trees	Both	Limited outliers	Supervised	Medium	Medium	High
Gradient Boosting	Both	Limited outliers	Supervised, ensemble	High	High	Low
Random Forests	Both	Messy & complex data	Supervised, ensemble	Medium	Medium – High	Low
SVM	Both	Messy & complex data	Supervised	High	Medium – High	Low
Perceptron	Both	Messy & complex data	Supervised	Medium	Medium – High	Low
Multi-layer Perceptron	Both	Messy & complex data, high volume	Supervised	High	High	Low

Table 10: Overview of popular algorithms used in machine learning

8) Predict

After devising an initial model using patterns extracted from the training data, the predict function is called on the test data to validate the model. In the case of regression problems, the predict function generates a numeric value such as price or a numeric indicator of correlation, and in the case of classification, the predict function is used to generate discrete classes, such as the movie category or spam/non-spam classification.

9) Evaluate

The next step is to evaluate the results. The method of evaluation will depend on the scope of your model, and specifically, whether it is a classification or regression model. In the case of classification, the common evaluation methods are the confusion matrix, classification report, and accuracy score.

$$\text{Accuracy} = \frac{\text{Number Predicted Correctly}}{\text{Number of Cases}}$$

Accuracy Score: This is a simple metric measuring how many cases the model classified correctly divided by the full number of cases. If all predictions are correct, the accuracy score is 1.0, and 0 if all cases are predicted incorrectly.

While accuracy alone is normally a reliable metric of performance, it may hide a lopsided number of false-positives or false-negatives. This isn't a problem if there's a balanced number of false-positives and false-negatives, but this isn't something we can ascertain using accuracy alone, which leads us to the following two evaluation methods.

Documentation for Accuracy Score: http://bit.ly/2OQ1jV7

Confusion Matrix: A confusion matrix, also known as an *error matrix*, is a simple table that summarizes the performance of the model, including the exact number of false-positives and false-negatives.

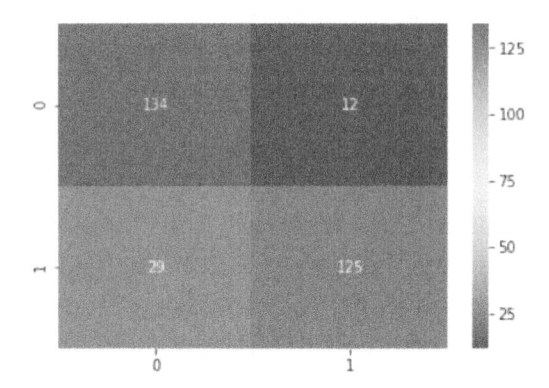

	0	1
0	134	12
1	29	125

Table 11: A confusion matrix generated using Seaborn

As seen in the top left box, the model in this example predicted 134 data points correctly as "0" and 125 cases correctly as "1". The model also mispredicted 12 data points as "1" and 29 cases as "0". This means that the 12 data points that were predicted "1" (false-positive) should have been classified as "0" and 29 data points predicted as "0" (false-negative) should have been classified as "1."

Using the confusion matrix, we can analyze the ratio of false-positives to false-negatives as well as calculate the final accuracy of the predictions via dividing the total of false-positive (12) and false-negatives (29) by the total number of data points, which in this case is 300.

(False-positives + False-negatives) / Total Data Points

(12 + 29) / 300 = 0.1366

The model misclassified 13.66% of data points, and if we take the complement of the percentage, we have the accuracy score of the model, which is 86.34%.

Documentation for Confusion Matrix: http://bit.ly/2YKC5vW

Classification Report: Another popular evaluation technique is the classification report, which generates three evaluation metrics as well as support.

	precision	recall	f1-score	support
0	0.97	0.94	0.95	63
1	0.96	0.98	0.97	108
avg / total	0.96	0.96	0.96	171

Figure 23: A classification report generated using Scikit-learn

a) **Precision** is the ratio of correctly predicted true-positives to the total of predicted positive cases. A high precision score translates to a low occurrence of false-positives.

$$\text{Precision} = \frac{\text{Number True Positives}}{\text{Number Predicted Positive Cases}}$$

This metric addresses the question of how accurate the model is when predicting a positive outcome? This, in other words, is the ability of the model not to label a negative case as positive, which is important in the case of drug tests, for example.

b) **Recall** is similar to precision but represents the ratio of correctly predicted true-positives to the total of actual positive cases. This metric addresses the question of how many positive outcomes were rightly classified as positive? This can be understood as the ability of the model to identify all positive cases.

Note that the numerator (top) is the same for both precision and recall, while the denominators (below) are different.

$$\text{Recall} = \frac{\text{Number True Positives}}{\text{Number Actual Positive Cases}}$$

c) **F1-score** is a weighted average of precision and recall. It's typically used as a metric for model-to-model comparison rather than for stand-alone model accuracy. In addition, the f1-score is generally lower than the accuracy score due to the way recall and precision are calculated.

d) **Support** is not an evaluation metric per se but rather a tally of the number of positive and negative cases respectively.

Documentation for Classification Report: http://bit.ly/2YDqKgV

In regards to evaluating regression problems (predicting continuous variables), the two most common measures are mean absolute error (MAE) and root mean square error (RMSE).

MAE measures the average of the errors in a set of predictions, i.e. how far the regression line is to the actual data points. RMSE, meanwhile, measures the standard deviation of the prediction errors, which informs how concentrated or spread out prediction errors are in relation to an optimal fit.

Given errors are squared before they are averaged, RMSE is far more sensitive to large errors than MAE. On the other hand, RMSE is not as easy to interpret as MAE as it doesn't describe the average error of the model's predictions. Subsequently, RMSE is used more as a feedback mechanism to penalize poor predictions rather than to investigate the average error for each prediction.

10) Optimize

The final step is to optimize the model. For clustering analysis techniques, this might mean going back and modifying the number of clusters, or changing the hyperparameters of a tree-based learning technique.

Model optimization can be performed manually using a trial and error system or via automation using a method like grid search. This particular technique allows you to trial a range of configurations for each hyperparameter and methodically test each of those possible hyperparameters. An automated voting process then takes place to determine the optimal model.

As the model must examine each possible combination of hyperparameters, grid search can take a long time to run (in line with the number of combinations you set for each hyperparameter). We will practice implementing grid search in Chapter 11.

QUIZ

1) The Python interpreter works:

a. from top to bottom through your code
b. through all your code in one single go
c. from the last line of your code up
d. from where you first call the algorithm

2) Which evaluation technique is likely to hide a lopsided number of false-positives or false-negatives?

a. Precision
b. F1-score
c. Accuracy
d. Confusion matrix

3) A confusion matrix evaluates classification models? True or False?

4) Which technique can we use to optimize an existing prediction model?

a. Grid search
b. *k*-means clustering
c. Precision

5) Exploratory data analysis is typically performed after which two steps?

a. Scrub data
b. Select algorithm
c. Import dataset
d. Import libraries

SOLUTIONS

1) a, From top to bottom through your code

2) c, Accuracy

3) True

4) a, Grid search

5) c & d, Import dataset & Import libraries

9

LINEAR REGRESSION

This chapter describes the code for building a supervised learning model to predict a numerical target variable using linear regression.

Linear regression, as you may know, plots a straight line or plane called the *hyperplane* that predicts the target value of data inputs by determining the dependence between the dependent variable (y) and its changing independent variables (X). In a p-dimensional space, a hyperplane is a subspace equivalent to dimension p−1. Thus, in a two-dimensional space, a hyperplane is a one-dimensional subspace/flat line. In a three-dimensional space, a hyperplane is effectively a two-dimensional subspace. Although it becomes difficult to visualize a hyperplane in four or more dimensions, the notion of a p−1 hyperplane also applies.

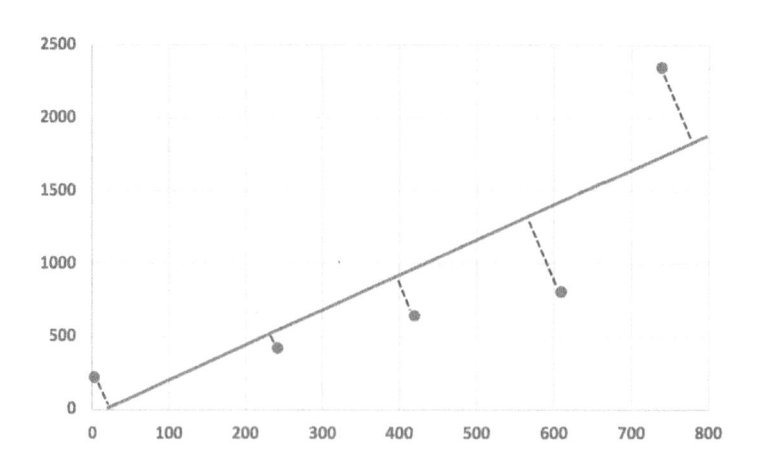

Figure 24: The distance of the data points to the hyperplane

The goal of the hyperplane is to dissect the known data points with minimal distance between itself and each data point. This means that if you were to draw a perpendicular line (90-degree angle) from the hyperplane to every data point on the plot, the distance of each data point would equate to the smallest possible distance of any potential hyperplane.

In preparation for building a linear regression model, we first need to remove or fill in missing values and confirm that the independent variables are those most correlated with the dependent variable. Those same independent variables, however, should not be correlated with each other. If a strong linear correlation exists between two or more independent variables, this leads to a problem called *collinearity* (in the case of two variables) or *multi-collinearity* (in the case of more than two correlated variables) where individual variables are not considered unique. While this doesn't affect the overall accuracy of the model, it affects the calculations and interpretation of individual (independent) variables. This means you can still reliably predict the output (dependent variable) using collinear variables, but it's difficult to say which variables are influential and which variables are redundant in deciding the model's outputs.

Exercise

To demonstrate this algorithm, we will code a linear regression model to predict house prices based on four independent variables. By adding the correlation coefficient for each independent variable with the y-intercept, we can then predict the value of the dependent variable (price).

The dataset used for this model is the Melbourne Housing Dataset, which contains data scraped from real estate property listings in Melbourne, Australia. The full dataset includes 21 variables including address, suburb, land size, number of rooms, price, longitude, latitude, postcode, etc.

The CSV file dataset can be downloaded from this link:
https://www.kaggle.com/anthonypino/melbourne-housing-market/#Melbourne_housing_FULL.csv

1) Import libraries
Let's begin by importing the following Python libraries.

```
import pandas as pd
import seaborn as sns
%matplotlib inline
from sklearn.model_selection import train_test_split
from sklearn.linear_model import LinearRegression
from sklearn import metrics
```

2) Import dataset
Using the Pandas `pd.read_csv` command, load the CSV dataset into a dataframe and assign the dataframe as a variable called `df` using the equals operator.

```
df = pd.read_csv('~/Downloads/Melbourne_housing_FULL.csv')
```

Feature	Data Type	Continuous/Discrete
Suburb	String	Discrete
Address	String	Discrete
Rooms	Integer	Continuous
Type	String	Discrete
Price	Integer	Continuous
Method	String	Discrete
SellerG (seller's name)	String	Discrete
Date	TimeDate	Discrete
Distance	Floating-point	Continuous
Postcode	Integer	Discrete
Bedroom2	Integer	Continuous
Bathroom	Integer	Continuous
Car	Integer	Continuous
Landsize	Integer	Continuous
BuildingArea	Integer	Continuous
YearBuilt	TimeDate	Discrete
CouncilArea	String	Discrete
Lattitude	String	Discrete
Longtitude	String	Discrete
Regionname	String	Discrete
Propertycount (in that suburb)	Integer	Continuous

Table 12: Melbourne housing dataset variables

Please note that the variables **Lattitude** and **Longtitude** are misspelled in this dataset, but this won't affect our code, as we'll remove these two variables in Step 3.

3) Remove variables

Regression models can be developed following the principle of parsimony[15] (using a limited or small number of variables that explain a large proportion of the variance) or capturing maximum variance (using more variables including variables that explain a small proportion of variance).[16] There are pros and cons to both methods, in addition to other considerations such as computational resources and model complexity.

---

[15] Also known as Occam's razor.
[16] Sarah Boslaugh, "Statistics in a Nutshell," *O'Reilly Media*, Second Edition, 2012.

For our model, we will focus on using a limited number of variables for reasons of convenience. We will also build our model using variables already expressed numerically, including **Price, Distance, BuildingArea, Bedroom2, Bathroom, Rooms, Car, Propertycount**, and **Landsize**. This means we can ignore and remove non-numerical variables such as **Address, Method, SellerG, Date**, etc., which would otherwise need to be transformed into a numerical format in order for the algorithm to read them.

```
del df['Address']
del df['Method']
del df['SellerG']
del df['Date']
del df['Postcode']
del df['YearBuilt']
del df['Type']
del df['Lattitude']
del df['Longtitude']
del df['Regionname']
del df['Suburb']
del df ['CouncilArea']
```

Let's use the `head` function to preview the dataframe.

```
df.head()
```

Run the model by right-clicking and selecting "Run" or navigating from the Jupyter Notebook menu: Cell > Run All.

```
10  del df['Address']
11  del df['Method']
12  del df['SellerG']
13  del df['Date']
14  del df['Postcode']
15  del df['YearBuilt']
16  del df['Type']
17  del df['Lattitude']
18  del df['Longtitude']
19  del df['Regionname']
20  del df['Suburb']
21  del df ['CouncilArea']
22
23  df.head()
24
```

	Rooms	Price	Distance	Bedroom2	Bathroom	Car	Landsize	BuildingArea	Propertycount
0	2	NaN	2.5	2.0	1.0	1.0	126.0	NaN	4019.0
1	2	1480000.0	2.5	2.0	1.0	1.0	202.0	NaN	4019.0
2	2	1035000.0	2.5	2.0	1.0	0.0	156.0	79.0	4019.0
3	3	NaN	2.5	3.0	2.0	1.0	0.0	NaN	4019.0
4	3	1465000.0	2.5	3.0	2.0	0.0	134.0	150.0	4019.0

As seen in the output above, we have removed more than half of the variables from the original dataframe. We can also see there's a high number of missing values in the form of NaN (not a number), which is common with real-life datasets. To inspect the full extent of missing values, we can use the `isnull().sum()` function.

```
df.isnull().sum()
```

Run the model in Jupyter Notebook.

```
24  df.isnull().sum()
```

```
Out[6]: Rooms              0
        Price           7610
        Distance           1
        Bedroom2        8217
        Bathroom        8226
        Car             8728
        Landsize       11810
        BuildingArea   21115
        Propertycount      3
        dtype: int64
```

The number of missing values ranges from as few as 1 (**Distance**) to as many as 21,115 in the case of **BuildingArea**. We'll discuss how to manage these missing values in the next section. For now, let's finish our exploratory analysis and use a heatmap to analyze the correlation (`corr`) between all variable combinations.

```
df_heat = df.corr()
sns.heatmap(df_heat,annot=True,cmap='coolwarm')
```

Run the model in Jupyter Notebook.

```
29  df_heat = df.corr()
30  sns.heatmap(df_heat,annot=True,cmap='coolwarm')
```

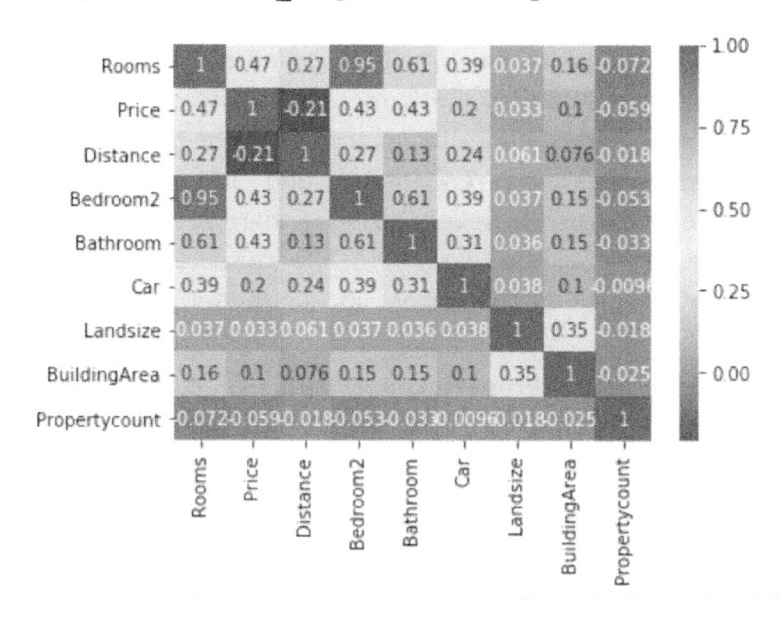

<matplotlib.axes._subplots.AxesSubplot at 0x1a17f09b00>

	Rooms	Price	Distance	Bedroom2	Bathroom	Car	Landsize	BuildingArea	Propertycount
Rooms	1	0.47	0.27	0.95	0.61	0.39	0.037	0.16	-0.072
Price	0.47	1	-0.21	0.43	0.43	0.2	0.033	0.1	-0.059
Distance	0.27	-0.21	1	0.27	0.13	0.24	0.061	0.076	-0.018
Bedroom2	0.95	0.43	0.27	1	0.61	0.39	0.037	0.15	-0.053
Bathroom	0.61	0.43	0.13	0.61	1	0.31	0.036	0.15	-0.033
Car	0.39	0.2	0.24	0.39	0.31	1	0.038	0.1	-0.009
Landsize	0.037	0.033	0.061	0.037	0.036	0.038	1	0.35	-0.018
BuildingArea	0.16	0.1	0.076	0.15	0.15	0.1	0.35	1	-0.025
Propertycount	-0.072	-0.059	-0.018	-0.053	-0.033	-0.0096	-0.018	-0.025	1

Lastly, let's inspect the shape of the dataset.

`df.shape`

Run the model in Jupyter Notebook.

Output: (34857, 9)

The output from `df.shape` shows the dataframe has 34,857 rows and 9 columns (features).

Other variables to remove

Bedroom2 is highly correlated with **Rooms** (0.95). As mentioned earlier, we want to avoid adding independent variables that are strongly correlated to each other. This means that we need to remove one of these two variables.

In terms of choosing which variable to remove, we can remove either variable depending on the knowledge we want to gain from our model. The variable **Bedroom2** (the second bedroom) might be useful for decision-making as it's more narrowly defined than **Rooms**. This explicit knowledge, for example, might be useful for making decisions regarding renovations and adding an extra bedroom to the property. However, because there are no missing values for the variable **Rooms**, and 8,226 missing values for **Bedroom2**, we will include the former in our model and remove the latter.

Landsize (0.033) and **Propertycount** (0.059) can also be removed as these variables show a low correlation to the dependent variable of **Price**, which is again undesirable for our linear regression model.

```
#Remove variables
del df ['Bedroom2']
del df ['Landsize']
del df ['Propertycount']
```

4) Remove or modify variables with missing values

Based on our exploratory data analysis, we know that missing values pose a problem with this dataset and especially as linear regression does not run smoothly with missing values. We therefore need to estimate or remove these values from the dataframe. The size of the dataframe, though, will be greatly reduced if we choose to remove all missing values on a row-by-row basis. The variable **BuildingArea**, for instance, has 21,115 missing rows, which makes up two-thirds of the dataframe!

To preserve row depth, we can remove this variable entirely, especially since it's not highly correlated with the dependent variable of **Price** (0.1).

The remaining variables can be removed on a row-by-row basis or filled with the mean value. Based on exploratory data analysis, we can:

a) Use the mean to fill variables with partial correlation to **Price** (i.e. **Car**)
b) Remove rows for variables with a small number of missing values (i.e. **Distance**)
c) Avoid filling values for variables with significant correlation to **Price** and instead remove those missing values row-by-row (i.e. **Bathroom**)

Variable	Missing Values	Correlation to Price	Action
Car	8728	0.2	Fill with mean
Landsize	11810	0.033	Remove variable
Distance	1	-0.21	Remove missing row
Propertycount	3	0.059	Remove variable
Bedroom2	8217	0.43	Remove variable
Bathroom	8226	0.43	Remove missing rows
BuildingArea	21115	0.1	Remove variable
Rooms	0	0.47	None
Price	7610	1	Remove missing rows

Table 13: Managing missing values

You'll notice that the default option for most variables is to remove the missing rows rather than to remove the entire variable or to artificially fill row values with the mean. The majority of the missing values appear in the same reoccurring rows, which means we'll have a hard time holding on to those rows unless we remove all the variables containing missing values.

To continue building our model, let's start the next round of code to fill or remove the missing values.

```
#Remove variable BuildingArea
del df ['BuildingArea']
```

```
#Fill in missing values with the mean for the variable Car
df['Car'].fillna(df['Car'].mean(),inplace=True)


#Drop remaining missing values on a row-by-row basis
df.dropna(axis=0, how='any', subset=None, inplace=True)
```

It's important to drop missing rows after removing **BuildingArea** and filling the missing values for **Car** as this will help to preserve more rows.

Let's now inspect the number of remaining rows in the dataframe.

```
df.shape
```

Run the model.

Output: (20800, 8)

We now have 20,800 rows or just over half of the original dataset, which is sufficient to build our linear regression model.

5) Set X and y variables

Next, let's assign our X and y variables. The X array contains the independent variables, and y is the dependent variable that we wish to predict (**Price**).

```
X = df[['Rooms', 'Distance', 'Bathroom', 'Car']]
y = df['Price']
```

Let's also shuffle and sub-divide the data into training and test sets using a standard 70/30 split. To make the results replicable in the future, we also need to control how the data is partitioned using a random seed number, which is set to "10" for this exercise.

```
X_train, X_test, y_train, y_test = train_test_split(X, y,
test_size=0.3, random_state=10, shuffle=True)
```

6) Set algorithm
Assign the Scikit-learn linear regression algorithm as a variable (i.e. **model** or **linear_reg**) using the equals operator. The naming of the variable isn't important as long as it's an intuitive description and fulfills the basic syntax for assigning variables in Python (i.e. no spaces, cannot begin with a number, etc.).

```
model = LinearRegression()
```

Use `fit` to link the training data to the algorithm stored in the variable **model**.

```
model.fit(X_train, y_train)
```

7) Find y-intercept and X coefficients
Using the following code, we can inspect the y-intercept of our model and the coefficients for each of the four independent variables. Note that you will need to run these two functions one-by-one (remove one function from the model to run the other) or run them in separate cells to view each output.

```
#Find y-intercept
model.intercept_
```

Run the model in Jupyter Notebook.

```
282725.3156777688
```

```
# Find x coefficients
model.coef_
```

Run the model.

```
array([269450.10790036, -37787.76622417, 207173.05927097,
47417.17159475])
```

Let's tidy up the X coefficients using a two-column table for easy reference.

```
model_results = pd.DataFrame(model.coef_, X.columns,
columns=['Coefficients'])
model_results
```

Run the model in Jupyter Notebook.

	Coefficients
Rooms	269450.107900
Distance	-37787.766224
Bathroom	207173.059271
Car	47417.171595

8) Predict

Let's now run the model to value an individual property by creating a new variable (new_house) using the following input features.

```
new_house = [
```

```
    2, #Rooms
    2.5, #Distance
    1, #Bathroom
    1, #Car
]

new_house_predict = model.predict([new_house])
new_house_predict
```
Run the model.

```
array([981746.34678378])
```

The predicted value of this house is AUD $981,746.347. The actual value of this house, according to the dataset, is AUD $1,480,000.

	Coefficient	new_house	Total
Rooms	269450.107900	2	538900.216
Distance	-37787.766224	2.5	-94469.416
Bathroom	207173.059271	1	207173.059
Car	47417.171595	1	47417.1716
y-intercept			282725.3156777688
Prediction (y)			981746.347

Table 14: Model calculations for predicting house value

9) Evaluate

Using mean absolute error from Scikit-learn, we can next compare the difference between the model's expected price predictions for the test set and the actual price.

```
prediction = model.predict(X_test)
metrics.mean_absolute_error(y_test, prediction)
```

Run the model.

363782.9423236326

The mean absolute error is 363782.9423236326, which means that on average, the model miscalculated the actual property listing's price by approximately $363,782.

As we removed 16 variables from the original dataset, this relatively high error rate is not unexpected. The **Type** (house, unit, or apartment) variable, for example, is a major indicator of house value—but as this variable is expressed non-numerically, we didn't include it in our model. We could, though, decide to rebuild the model and convert **Type** into numeric variables using one-hot encoding.

Also, while linear regression is extremely fast to run, it's not known for prediction accuracy and there are more reliable algorithms out there, as we will cover in the following chapters.

For more information about linear regression, Scikit-learn provides detailed documentation for this algorithm including a practical code example. Please note, though, that the documentation does not demonstrate linear regression using split validation (training and test split) as demonstrated in this chapter.

Documentation for Linear Regression: http://bit.ly/2Z0SmvK

QUIZ

1) It's important for the independent variables to be strongly correlated with the dependent variable and one or more of the other independent variables. True or False?

2) Linear regression can be used for predicting:

a. Species of penguins
b. Fraudulent transactions
c. Groups of customers
d. House prices

3) Linear regression can be used even if the dataset has missing values. True or False?

4) Which evaluation technique can we use to evaluate the performance of a regression model?

a. Classification report
b. Mean absolute error
c. Accuracy
d. Confusion matrix

5) What is the price of a three-bedroom house with a y-intercept of 100,000 and a coefficient of 100,000 for each bedroom?

a. 400,000
b. 300,000
c. 100,000
d. 500,000

SOLUTIONS

1) False (Ideally, the independent variables should not be strongly correlated with each other.)

2) d, House price

3) False (The linear regression algorithm does not run with missing values.)

4) b, Mean absolute error

5) a, 400,000

10

LOGISTIC REGRESSION

Machine learning generally involves predicting a quantitative outcome or a qualitative class. The former is commonly referred to as a regression problem, and in the case of linear regression, this involves predicting a numeric outcome based on the input of continuous variables. When predicting a qualitative outcome (class), the task is considered a classification problem. Examples of classification problems include predicting what products a user will buy or predicting if a target user will click on an online advertisement (True/False).

Not all algorithms, though, fit cleanly into this simple dichotomy and logistic regression is a notable example. Logistic regression is part of the regression family because, as with linear regression, it involves predicting outcomes based on analyzing quantitative relationships between variables. But unlike linear regression, it accepts both continuous and discrete variables as input and its output is qualitative; it predicts a discrete class such as Yes/No or Customer/Non-customer.

In practice, the logistic regression algorithm analyzes relationships between variables and assigns probabilities to discrete outcomes using the Sigmoid function, which converts numerical results into an expression of probability between 0 and 1.0.

A value of 0 represents no chance of occurring, whereas 1 represents a certain chance of occurring. For binary predictions, we can assign two discrete classes with a cut-off point of 0.5. Anything above 0.5 is classified as class A and anything below 0.5 is classified as class B.

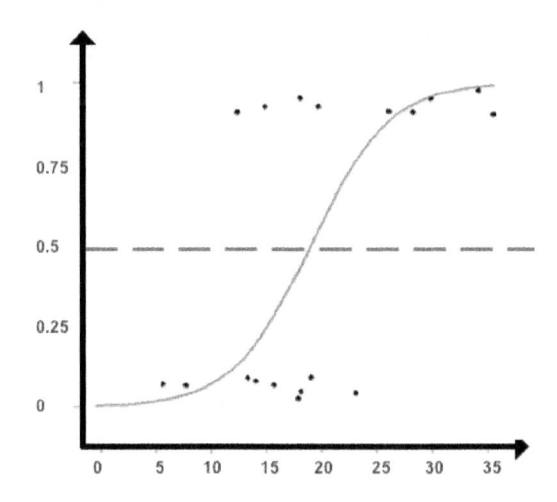

Figure 25: A sigmoid function used to classify data points

After assigning data points to a class using the Sigmoid function, a hyperplane is used as a decision boundary to split the two classes (to the best of its ability). The decision boundary can then be used to predict the class of future data points.

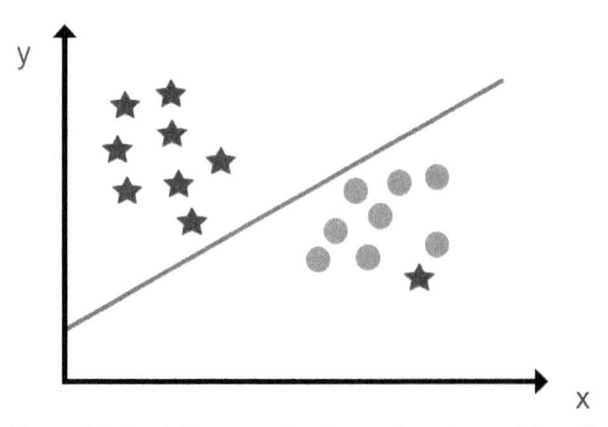

Figure 26: Logistic regression hyperplane is used to split the two classes

Logistic regression can also be used to classify multiple outcomes but is generally used for binary classification (predicting one of two discrete classes). Other techniques including the Naive

Bayes' classifier and support vector machines (SVM) are considered to be more effective at classifying multiple discrete outcomes.

Exercise

In this next code exercise, we will use logistic regression to predict the outcome of a Kickstarter campaign, and specifically, whether the campaign will reach its target funding in the form of a binary "0" (No) or "1" (Yes) output. Kickstarter.com is an online crowd-funding platform for creative projects and new products.

1) Import libraries

The libraries used for this exercise are Pandas, Seaborn, Matplotlib and Pyplot (a MATLAB-like plotting framework that combines Pyplot with NumPy), as well as Scikit-learn.

```
import pandas as pd
import matplotlib.pyplot as plt
import seaborn as sns
%matplotlib inline
from sklearn.model_selection import train_test_split
from sklearn.linear_model import LogisticRegression
from sklearn.metrics import confusion_matrix, classification_report
```

2) Import dataset

The next important step is to import the CSV dataset into Jupyter Notebook as a Pandas dataframe after downloading it from https://www.kaggle.com/tayoaki/kickstarter-dataset.

```
df = pd.read_csv('~/Downloads/18k_Projects.csv')
```

Feature	Data Type	Continuous/Discrete
ID	Integer	Discrete
Name	String	Discrete
URL	String	Discrete
State	String	Discrete
Currency	String	Discrete
Top_category	String	Discrete
Category	String	Discrete
Creator	String	Discrete
Location	String	Discrete
Updates	Integer	Continuous
Comments	Integer	Continuous
Rewards	Integer	Continuous
Goal	Integer	Continuous
Pledged	Integer	Continuous
Backers	Integer	Continuous
Start	TimeDate	Discrete
End	TimeDate	Discrete
Duration in Days	Integer	Continuous
Facebook Connected	Boolean	Discrete
Facebook Friends	Integer	Continuous
Facebook Shares	Integer	Continuous
Has Video	Boolean	Discrete
Latitude	String	Discrete
Longitude	String	Discrete
Start Timestamp (UTC)	TimeDate	Discrete
End Timestamp (UTC)	TimeDate	Discrete
Creator Bio	String	Discrete
Creator Website	String	Discrete
Creator - # Projects Created	Integer	Continuous
Creator - # Projects Backed	Integer	Continuous
# Videos	Integer	Continuous
# Images	Integer	Continuous
# Words (Description)	Integer	Continuous
# Words (Risks and Challenges)	Integer	Continuous
# FAQs	Integer	Continuous

Table 15: Kickstarter Projects dataset

3) Remove variables

Step three is to remove non-essential variables using the delete function.

```
del df ['Id']
del df ['Name']
del df ['Url']
del df ['Location']
```

```
del df ['Pledged']
del df ['Creator']
del df ['Category']
del df ['Updates']
del df ['Start']
del df ['End']
del df ['Latitude']
del df ['Longitude']
del df ['Start Timestamp (UTC)']
del df ['End Timestamp (UTC)']
del df ['Creator Bio']
del df ['Creator Website']
```

This removes 16 variables from the dataframe. Some variables were removed because they are strings or timestamps that cannot be parsed and interpreted as numeric values by the logistic regression algorithm. Not all non-numeric variables were removed, as we'll be transforming some of these variables using one-hot encoding in Step 4.

4) Convert non-numeric values

Logistic regression accepts discrete variables as input, provided they are expressed numerically. Consequently, we need to convert the remaining categorical features into numeric values using one-hot encoding.

```
df = pd.get_dummies(df, columns=['State', 'Currency', 'Top Category', 'Facebook Connected', 'Has Video'], drop_first = True)
```

Finally, let's inspect the shape of the dataframe for future reference.

```
df.shape
```

Run the model.

Output: (18142, 36)

The dataframe has 18,142 rows and 36 columns/features.

5) Remove and fill in missing values
Let's now inspect the dataframe for missing values.

```
df.isnull().sum()
```

Run the model.

```
Comments                            0    Currency_NZD                   0
Rewards                             0    Currency_USD                   0
Goal                                0    Top Category_Comics            0
Backers                             0    Top Category_Crafts            0
Duration in Days                    0    Top Category_Dance             0
Facebook Friends                 5852    Top Category_Design            0
Facebook Shares                     0    Top Category_Fashion           0
Creator - # Projects Created        0    Top Category_Film & Video      0
Creator - # Projects Backed      4244    Top Category_Food              0
# Videos                          101    Top Category_Games             0
# Images                            0    Top Category_Journalism        0
# Words (Description)               0    Top Category_Music             0
# Words (Risks and Challenges)    101    Top Category_Photography       0
# FAQs                              0    Top Category_Publishing        0
State_successful                    0    Top Category_Technology        0
Currency_CAD                        0    Top Category_Theater           0
Currency_EUR                        0    Facebook Connected_Yes         0
Currency_GBP                        0    Has Video_Yes                  0
```

The output shows that four of the 36 variables contain missing values. These four variables and their correlation to the y (dependent) variable (**State_successful**) are summarized in Table 16.

```
#Code for obtaining correlation coefficients
df['State_successful'].corr(df['Facebook Friends'])
df['State_successful'].corr(df['Creator - # Projects Backed'])
df['State_successful'].corr(df['# Videos'])
```

```
df['State_successful'].corr(df['# Words (Risks and Challenges)'])
```

Variable	Missing	Correlation to y	Suggested Action
Facebook Friends	5852	0.160	Fill with Mean
Creator - # Projects Backed	4244	0.106	Fill with Mean
# Videos	101	0.056579190784304276	Remove missing rows
# Words (Risks and Challenges)	101	0.007544860569767823	Remove missing rows

Table 16: Summary of variables with missing values

The variables **Facebook Friends** and **Creator - # Projects Backed** have a high number of missing values but their correlation to the dependent variable (**State_successful**) is significant for analysis. Removing rows containing missing values from these two variables would also cut the dataset in half (from 18,142 rows to 9,532 rows).

Regarding the other two variables, we can remove the missing rows given their low frequency (101). Alternatively, you could opt to remove these two variables given their low correlation with the dependent variable.

Next, let's use the `describe()` method to inspect the standard deviation and range of the two remaining variables.

```
df.describe()
```

	Backers	Duration in Days	Facebook Friends	Facebook Shares	Creator - # Projects Created	Creator - # Projects Backed
count	18142.000000	18142.000000	12290.000000	18142.000000	18142.000000	13898.000000
mean	138.070279	31.398468	694.233686	396.729137	1.520119	5.149950
std	633.787780	10.058827	783.802343	2544.711314	2.540474	20.351979
min	1.000000	1.000000	0.000000	0.000000	1.000000	0.000000
25%	7.000000	29.000000	216.250000	21.000000	1.000000	0.000000
50%	29.000000	30.000000	453.000000	104.000000	1.000000	1.000000
75%	89.000000	32.000000	860.000000	322.000000	1.000000	4.000000
max	35383.000000	60.000000	4885.000000	260505.000000	111.000000	1205.000000

The standard deviation (std) and range (max – min) for the variable **Facebook Friends** are high but much lower for the variable **Creator - # Projects Backed**.

Let's take one final look at these variables using a distribution plot using Seaborn and Matplotlib/Pyplot.

```
#Distribution plot of variable 'Facebook Friends'
plt.figure(figsize=(12,6))
sns.distplot(df['Facebook Friends'], kde=True, hist=0)
```

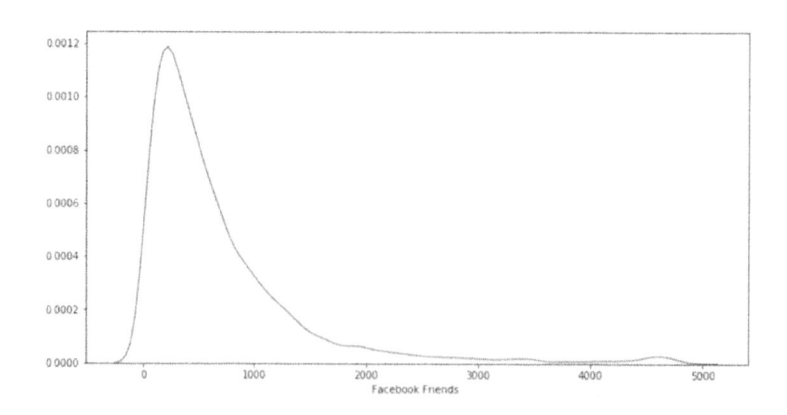

```
#Distribution plot of variable 'Creator - # Projects Backed'
```

```
plt.figure(figsize=(12,6))
sns.distplot(df['Creator - # Projects Backed'], kde=True, hist=0)
```

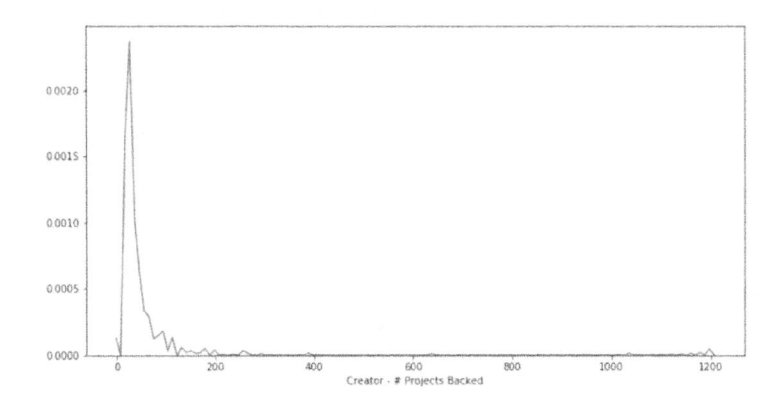

Owing to high variance, it's challenging to fill the variable **Facebook Friends** with the mean, mode, or another artificial value, as none of these methods provide a reliable fill value. Also, due to the significant correlation of this variable to the dependent variable, we don't necessarily want to remove it from the model. We'll therefore proceed by retaining this variable and removing rows with missing values.

We have a similar problem with the variable **Creator - # Projects Backed**, but due to its lower range, standard deviation, and correlation to the dependent variable, we can fill this variable with the mean without significantly altering patterns in the data.

```
# Fill in missing values for 'Creator - # Projects Backed' with the
mean value
df['Creator - # Projects Backed'].fillna(df['Creator - # Projects
Backed'].mean(), inplace=True)

# Drop remaining missing values for remaining variables
df.dropna(axis=0, how='any', subset=None, inplace=True)
```

```
df.shape
```

Run the model.

Output: (12215, 36)

Following these alterations, we have 12,215 rows, equivalent to two-thirds of the original dataset.

6) Set X and y variables

The dependent variable (y) for this model is the binary variable **State_successful**.

The remaining variables are the independent variables (X). Rather than calling each variable in the code separately as performed in the previous exercise, we can call the full dataframe and remove the y variable using the `drop` method.

```
X = df.drop('State_successful',axis=1)
y = df['State_successful']
```

Shuffle and split data 70/30.

```
X_train, X_test, y_train, y_test = train_test_split(X, y,
test_size=0.3, random_state=10, shuffle=True)
```

7) Set algorithm

Assign `LogisticRegression()` to the variable **model** or a variable name of your choosing.

```
model = LogisticRegression()
```

Fit the algorithm to the training data.

```
model.fit(X_train, y_train)
```

8) Evaluate

Using the `predict` function on the `x_test` data, let's compare the predicted results with the actual outcome of the `y_test` set using a confusion matrix and classification report from Scikit-learn.

```
model_predict = model.predict(X_test)


#Confusion matrix
print(confusion_matrix(y_test, model_predict))


#Classification report
print(classification_report(y_test, model_predict))
```

```
[[1658  171]
 [ 211 1625]]
             precision    recall  f1-score   support

          0       0.89      0.91      0.90      1829
          1       0.90      0.89      0.89      1836

avg / total       0.90      0.90      0.90      3665
```

The confusion matrix indicates that we had 171 false-positive predictions and 211 false-negative predictions. The overall performance of the model, though, is favorable when we consider the high precision, recall, and f1-score conveyed in the classification report.

9) Predict

Let's now use our model to predict the likely outcome of an individual Kickstarter campaign based on the input of its independent variables.

```
new_project = [
        0, #Comments
        9, #Rewards
        2500, #Goal
        157, #Backers
        31, #Duration in Days
        319, #Facebook Friends
        110, #Facebook Shares
        1, #Creator - # Projects Created
        0, #Creator - # Projects Backed
        0, ## Videos
        12, ## Images
        872, ## Words (Description)
        65, ## Words (Risks and Challenges)
        0, ## FAQs
        0, #Currency_AUD
        1, #Currency_CAD
        0, #Currency_EUR
        0, #Currency_GBP
        0, #Currency_NZD
        0, #Currency_USD
        0, #Top Category_Art
        0, #Top Category_Comics
        0, #Top Category_Crafts
        0, #Top Category_Dance
        0, #Top Category_Design
        0, #Top Category_Fashion
        1, #Top Category_Film & Video
        0, #Top Category_Food
        0, #Top Category_Games
        0, #Top Category_Journalism
```

```
    0, #Top Category_Music
    0, #Top Category_Photography
    0, #Top Category_Publishing
    0, #Top Category_Technology
    0, #Top Category_Theater
    0, #Facebook Connected_No
    0, #Facebook Connected_Yes
    0, #Has Video_No
    1, #Has Video_Yes
]
```

You can generate the section of code above manually or you may like to use a temporary code shortcut included in Appendix 2 of this book.

Let's now call `predict` on the model using the `new_project` as new input data.

```
new_pred = model.predict([new_project])
new_pred
```

Run the model.

Output: `array([1], dtype=uint8)`

According to the positive binary outcome of our model [1], the new campaign is predicted to reach its target funding based on its input variables and the rules of our model. A negative binary outcome of [0], meanwhile, would classify the campaign as unsuccessful.

Documentation for Logistic Regression: http://bit.ly/2N0DXcu

QUIZ

1) We need to build a prediction model to predict the sex of five different species of penguins based on their weight, height, and color. How many output variables will our model have?

a. 3
b. 2
c. 5
d. 1

2) Logistic regression can be used interchangeably with linear regression to predict the same output variable. True or False?

3) How many false-positives did the model produce based on the results of the confusion matrix?

a. 1658
b. 171
c. 211
d. 1625

4) Which function can we use to apply our trained model to new data in order to produce a prediction?

a. test()
b. head()
c. predict()
d. print()

5) Logistic regression excels at:

a. Binary classification
b. Reducing the number of components
c. Predicting a high number of discrete categories
d. Visualizing data patterns

SOLUTIONS

1) b, 2

2) False (Logistic regression is a classification technique, whereas linear regression is a regression technique that predicts a continuous and numerical value)

3) b, 171

4) c, predict()

5) a, Binary classification

SUPPORT VECTOR MACHINES

In this chapter, we discuss a relatively new regression analysis technique called *support vector machines*, or *SVM* for short. SVM is considered one of the best classifiers in supervised learning for analyzing complex data and downplaying the influence of outliers. Developed within the computer science community in the 1990s, SVM was initially designed for predicting numeric and categorical outcomes as a double-barrel prediction technique. Today, SVM is mostly used as a classification technique for predicting categorical outcomes—similar to logistic regression.

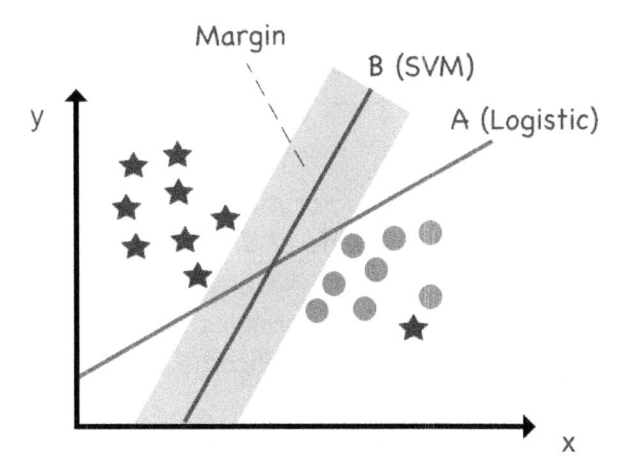

Figure 27: Logistic regression versus SVM

In binary prediction scenarios, SVM mirrors logistic regression as it attempts to separate classes based on the mathematical relationship between variables. Unlike logistic regression, however, SVM attempts to separate data classes from a position of maximum distance between itself and the partitioned data points. Its key feature is the *margin*, which is the distance between the boundary line and the nearest data point, multiplied by two. The margin provides support to cope with new data points and outliers that would otherwise infringe on a logistic regression boundary line.

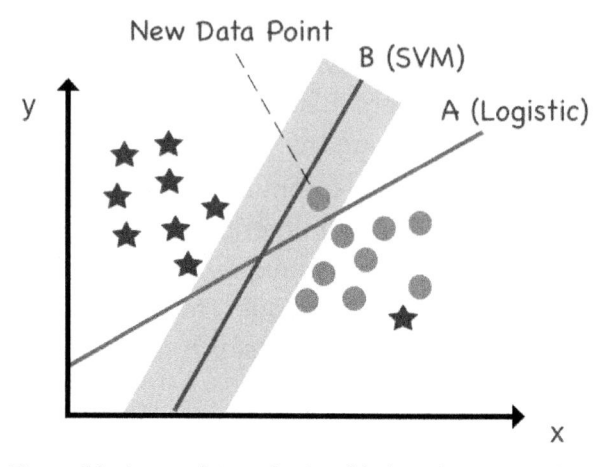

Figure 28: A new data point is added to the scatterplot

Exercise

In this chapter we will use the support vector machines algorithm as a binary classifier to predict the outcome of a user clicking on an online advertisement. Using the Advertising dataset introduced in Chapter 6, the model's input variables include Age, Male (sex), Daily Time Spent On Site, Area Income, and Daily Internet Usage.

1) Import libraries

We will be using SVC (Support Vector Classifier) from the Scikit-learn library to implement this model and evaluating the predictions using a classification report and a confusion matrix. We will later optimize the model using grid search.

```
import pandas as pd
from sklearn.model_selection import train_test_split
from sklearn.svm import SVC
from sklearn.metrics import classification_report, confusion_matrix
from sklearn.model_selection import GridSearchCV
```

2) Import dataset

Use `pd.read_csv` to import the Advertising dataset.

```
df = pd.read_csv('~/Downloads/advertising.csv')
```

3) Remove variables

Next, remove the following two variables from the dataframe.

```
del df ['Ad Topic Line']
del df ['Timestamp']
```

4) Convert non-numeric variables

Using one-hot encoding, convert **Country** and **City** variables to numeric values.

```
df = pd.get_dummies(df, columns=['Country','City'])
```

5) Set X and y variables

Assign **Clicked on Ad** as the y target variable and the remaining variables as X.

```
X = df.drop('Clicked on Ad',axis=1)
y = df['Clicked on Ad']
```

Split the data into training and test tests.

```
X_train, X_test, y_train, y_test = train_test_split(X, y,
test_size=0.3, random_state=10)
```

6) Set algorithm

Assign a new variable to Scikit-learn's SVC (support vector classifier) algorithm. Note that for regression problems, you will need to use SVR (support vector regression) from Scikit-learn.[17]

```
model = SVC()
```

Fit the algorithm to the training data.

```
model.fit(X_train, y_train)
```

7) Evaluate

Assign a new variable to the prediction of the X test data using the model created in Step 6.

```
model_predict = model.predict(X_test)
```

Next, generate a confusion matrix and classification report to evaluate the results of the model using the test input data (`X_test`) contained in `model_predict` against the true output (`y_test`).

```
#Confusion matrix
print(confusion_matrix(y_test, model_predict))

#Classification report
print(classification_report(y_test, model_predict))
```

---

[17] For more information about SVR, please see https://scikit-learn.org/stable/modules/generated/sklearn.svm.SVR.html

Run the model.

```
#Confusion matrix
print(confusion_matrix(y_test, model_predict))

#Classification report
print(classification_report(y_test, model_predict))
```

```
[[124  22]
 [ 68  86]]
              precision    recall  f1-score   support

           0       0.65      0.85      0.73       146
           1       0.80      0.56      0.66       154

    accuracy                           0.70       300
   macro avg       0.72      0.70      0.70       300
weighted avg       0.72      0.70      0.69       300
```

The current performance of the model isn't as accurate as we might hope. The confusion matrix reports a high occurrence of false-negatives (68), and the classification report states that precision, recall, and the f1-score are all below 0.75.

8) Grid search

We can improve the accuracy of our model using a special technique called *grid search* to help us find the optimal hyperparameters for this algorithm. While there are many hyperparameters belonging to SVC, we will focus on C and gamma, which generally have the biggest impact on prediction accuracy using this algorithm.

The hyperparameter C controls the cost of misclassification on the training data. In other words, C regulates the extent to which misclassified cases (placed on the wrong side of the margin) are ignored. This flexibility in the model is referred to as a "soft margin" and ignoring cases that cross over the soft margin can lead to a better fit. In practice, the lower C is, the more errors the soft margin is permitted to ignore. A C value of '0' enforces no penalty on misclassified cases.

Gamma refers to the Gaussian radial basis function and the influence of the support vector. In general, a small gamma produces high bias and low variance models. Conversely, a large gamma leads to low bias and high variance in the model.

Grid search allows us to list a range of values to test for each hyperparameter. An automated voting process then takes place to determine the optimal value for each hyperparameter. Note that as grid search must examine each combination of hyperparameters, it can take a long time to run and particularly as you add more values for testing. In this exercise, we will test three values for each hyperparameter.

The following code should be used in a new cell within the same notebook.

Begin by stating the hyperparameters you wish to test.

```
hyperparameters = {'C':[10,25,50],'gamma':[0.001,0.0001,0.00001]}
```

Link your specified hyperparameters to GridSearchCV and the SVC algorithm under a new variable name.

```
grid = GridSearchCV(SVC(),hyperparameters)
```

Next, fit grid search to the X and y training data.

```
grid.fit(X_train, y_train)
```

We can now use the `grid.best_params_` function to review the optimal combination of hyperparameters. This may take 30 seconds or longer to run on your machine.

`grid.best_params_`

```
1  hyperparameters = {'C':[10,25,50],'gamma':[0.001,0.0001,0.00001]}
2  grid = GridSearchCV(SVC(), hyperparameters)
3
4  grid.fit(X_train, y_train)
5
6  grid.best_params_
7
```

`{'C': 50, 'gamma': 1e-05}`

After testing each possible permutation provided for C and Gamma, grid search has found that 50 for C and 0.0001 for gamma are the ideal hyperparameters for this model.

9) Grid search predict

Let's link the test data with the model using the new hyperparameters supplied by grid search, and review the prediction results inside a new cell.

`grid_predictions = grid.predict(X_test)`

```
#Confusion matrix
print(confusion_matrix(y_test,grid_predictions))


#Classification report
print(classification_report(y_test,grid_predictions))
```

Run the model.

```
1  grid_predictions = grid.predict(X_test)
2
3  #Confusion matrix
4  print(confusion_matrix(y_test,grid_predictions))
5
6  #Classification report
7  print(classification_report(y_test,grid_predictions))
8
9
```

```
[[129  17]
 [ 15 139]]
             precision    recall  f1-score   support

          0       0.90      0.88      0.89       146
          1       0.89      0.90      0.90       154

avg / total       0.89      0.89      0.89       300
```

As evidenced in the confusion matrix and classification report, the new hyperparameters have improved the prediction performance of this model, with an almost evenly split number of false-positives (17) and false-negatives (15), and 0.89 for precision, recall, and f1-score.

Documentation for SVC: http://bit.ly/2YYxfdy

Documentation for Grid Search: http://bit.ly/2P6tq2v

QUIZ

1) What is the margin?

a. The middle of the dataset
b. The classification boundary line
c. The distance between the boundary line and the nearest data point
d. A scatterplot axis

2) Support vector machines can be used for:

a. Regression only
b. Classification only
c. Classification and regression
d. Clustering

3) Support vector machines are more effective at classifying multiple discrete outcomes than logistic regression. True or False?

4) What is the name of the classification version of support vector machines in Scikit-learn?

a. SVClassification()
b. SVC()
c. SVR()
d. SVC(1)

5) What is a feature of a soft margin?

a. Ignoring data points that cross over into the margin
b. No leeway for data points that cross over into the margin
c. A very narrow margin

d. A very wide margin

6) In general, a small gamma produces:

a. Low bias and low variance models
b. High bias and low variance models
c. Low bias and high variance models
d. High bias and high variance models

SOLUTIONS

1) c. The distance between the boundary line and the nearest data point

2) c, Classification and regression

3) True

4) b, SVC()

5) a, Ignoring data points that cross over into the margin

6) b, High bias and low variance models

12

k-NEAREST NEIGHBORS

Our next supervised learning classification technique is *k*-nearest neighbors, which classifies new unknown data points based on their proximity to known data points. This process of classification is determined by setting "*k*" number of data points closest to the target data point. If we set *k* to 3, for example, *k*-NN analyzes the nearest three data points (neighbors) to the target data point.

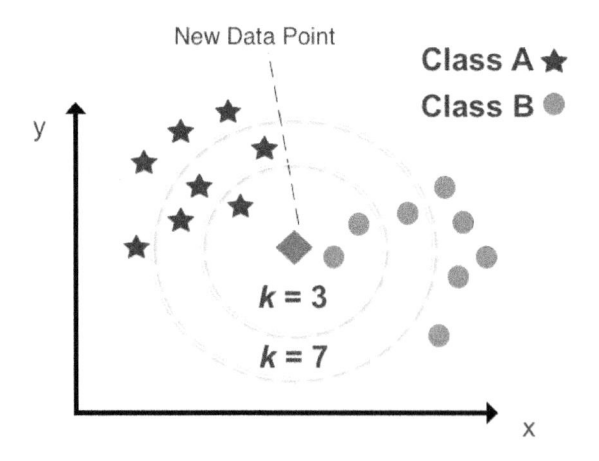

Figure 29: An example of *k*-NN clustering used to predict the class of a new data point

The *k*-nearest neighbors technique is sometimes referred to as a "memory-based procedure" because the full training data is used each time a prediction is made.[18] For this reason, *k*-NN is generally not recommended for analyzing large datasets and measuring multiple distances in high-dimensional data. Reducing the number of dimensions, through the use of a descending dimension algorithm such as principal component analysis (PCA) or by merging variables, is a common strategy to simplify and prepare a dataset for *k*-NN analysis.

Exercise

In the following code exercise, we will practice using *k*-nearest neighbors to predict the outcome of a user clicking on an online advertisement based on the class of nearby data points.

1) Import libraries

This model is built using the `KNeighborsClassifier` from Scikit-learn. We'll also be relying on `StandardScaler` to standardize the data, as we did earlier with principal component analysis.

```
import pandas as pd
from sklearn.preprocessing import StandardScaler
from sklearn.model_selection import train_test_split
from sklearn.neighbors import KNeighborsClassifier
from sklearn.metrics import classification_report, confusion_matrix
```

2) Import dataset

For this exercise, we are again using the Advertising dataset.

```
df = pd.read_csv('~/Downloads/advertising.csv')
```

3) Remove variables

---

[18] Gareth James, Daniela Witten & Trevor Hastie Robert Tibshirani, "An Introduction to Statistical Learning with Applications in R," *Springer*, 2017.

Next, we'll remove the discrete variables from the dataframe, including **Ad Topic Line**, **Timestamp**, **Male**, **Country**, and **City**. k-NN generally works best with continuous variables such as age and area income.

```
del df ['Ad Topic Line']
del df ['Timestamp']
del df['Male']
del df ['Country']
del df ['City']
```

Let's preview the updated dataframe and the remaining variables using the `head` command.

```
df.head()
```

Run the model.

```
1  import pandas as pd
2  from sklearn.preprocessing import StandardScaler
3  from sklearn.model_selection import train_test_split
4  from sklearn.neighbors import KNeighborsClassifier
5  from sklearn.metrics import classification_report, confusion_matrix
6
7  df = pd.read_csv('~/Downloads/advertising.csv')
8
9  del df ['Ad Topic Line']
10 del df ['Timestamp']
11 del df['Male']
12 del df ['Country']
13 del df ['City']
14
15 df.head()
16
```

	Daily Time Spent on Site	Age	Area Income	Daily Internet Usage	Clicked on Ad
0	68.95	35	61833.90	256.09	0
1	80.23	31	68441.85	193.77	0
2	69.47	26	59785.94	236.50	0
3	74.15	29	54806.18	245.89	0
4	68.37	35	73889.99	225.58	0

4) Scale data

Given that the scale of variables has a major impact on the output of this algorithm, we'll use `StandardScaler()` from Scikit-learn to standardize the variance of the independent variables (while dropping the dependent variable **Clicked on Ad**). This transformation will help to avoid one or more variables with a high range unfairly pulling the focus of the model.

```
scaler = StandardScaler()
scaler.fit(df.drop('Clicked on Ad',axis=1))
scaled_features = scaler.transform(df.drop('Clicked on Ad',axis=1))
```

5) Set X and y values

Assign X and y variables, with the standardized independent variables assigned as X and the dependent variable of **Clicked on Ad** as y.

```
X = scaled_features
y = df['Clicked on Ad']
```

We'll again use a standard 70/30 split with a `test_size` of 0.3 and `random_state` bookmarked as 10.

```
X_train, X_test, y_train, y_test = train_test_split(X, y,
test_size=0.3, random_state=10, shuffle=True)
```

6) Set algorithm

Assign and configure the *k*-NN algorithm to an initial number of neighbors, which in this case is matched to reflect the default number for this algorithm (5). Note that setting *k* to an uneven number helps to eliminate the possibility of a prediction stalemate in the case of a binary prediction.

```
model = KNeighborsClassifier(n_neighbors=5)
```

Fit the algorithm to the training data.

```
model.fit(X_train, y_train)
```

7) Evaluate

Using the `predict` function, we can compare the model's predictions for the test data against the y test data to evaluate the accuracy of the model.

```
model_predict = model.predict(X_test)
```

```
print(confusion_matrix(y_test, model_predict))
print(classification_report(y_test, model_predict))
```

Run the model.

```
[[144   2]
 [ 10 144]]
             precision    recall  f1-score   support

          0       0.94      0.99      0.96       146
          1       0.99      0.94      0.96       154

avg / total       0.96      0.96      0.96       300
```

The model returns favorable results with a low number of false-positives (2) and false-negatives (10), and an f1-score of 0.96.

8) Optimize

We can now experiment with the number of neighbors chosen in step 5 and attempt to reduce the number of incorrectly predicted outcomes.

n_neighbors	False-positives	False-negatives	Total
3	3	9	12
4	2	11	13
7	3	10	13
15	3	11	14
25	2	12	14
31	2	13	15

Table 17: Results from different n_neighbors combinations

Based on manual trial and error, we can improve the model by opting for 3 neighbors.

9) Predict

As the final step of this exercise, we can deploy our model (n_neighbors=3) on the first 10 rows of the scaled_features dataframe to predict the likely outcome.

```
model.predict(scaled_features)[0:10]
```

```
23
24  model = KNeighborsClassifier(n_neighbors=3)
25
26  model.fit(X_train, y_train)
27
28  model_predict = model.predict(X_test)
29
30  #print(confusion_matrix(y_test, model_predict))
31  #print(classification_report(y_test, model_predict))
32
33  model.predict(scaled_features)[0:10]
```

```
array([0, 0, 0, 0, 0, 0, 0, 1, 0, 0])
```

Based on the nearest 3 neighbors, only one user is expected to click on the advertisement (1) according to our prediction model. As we can expect, the model's predictions are accurate if we compare the results with the data used for training.

```
9
10  df.head(10)
11
```

	Daily Time Spent on Site	Age	Area Income	Daily Internet Usage	Ad Topic Line	City	Male	Country	Timestamp	Clicked on Ad
0	68.95	35	61833.90	256.09	Cloned 5thgeneration orchestration	Wrightburgh	0	Tunisia	2016-03-27 00:53:11	0
1	80.23	31	68441.85	193.77	Monitored national standardization	West Jodi	1	Nauru	2016-04-04 01:39:02	0
2	69.47	26	59785.94	236.50	Organic bottom-line service-desk	Davidton	0	San Marino	2016-03-13 20:35:42	0
3	74.15	29	54806.18	245.89	Triple-buffered reciprocal time-frame	West Terrifurt	1	Italy	2016-01-10 02:31:19	0
4	68.37	35	73889.99	225.58	Robust logistical utilization	South Manuel	0	Iceland	2016-06-03 03:36:18	0
5	59.99	23	59761.56	226.74	Sharable client-driven software	Jamieberg	1	Norway	2016-05-19 14:30:17	0
6	88.91	33	53852.85	208.36	Enhanced dedicated support	Brandonstad	0	Myanmar	2016-01-28 20:59:32	0
7	66.00	48	24593.33	131.76	Reactive local challenge	Port Jefferybury	1	Australia	2016-03-07 01:40:15	1
8	74.53	30	68862.00	221.51	Configurable coherent function	West Colin	1	Grenada	2016-04-18 09:33:42	0
9	69.88	20	55642.32	183.82	Mandatory homogeneous architecture	Ramirezton	1	Ghana	2016-07-11 01:42:51	0

Documentation for k-NN: http://bit.ly/31wc6oC

QUIZ

1) Using Scikit-learn, the default number of variables using the KNeighborsClassifier is:

a. 5
b. 3
c. 4
d. 1

2) Which of the following evaluation techniques can we use to evaluate the accuracy of a *k*-nearest neighbors model?

a. Classification report
b. Mean absolute error
c. Elbow method
d. Grid search

3) Which metric can we use to compare the accuracy of different *k*-NN models?

a. Support
b. f1 score
c. Precision
d. Accuracy

4) Which algorithm is sometimes used to simplify and prepare a dataset for *k*-NN analysis?

a. Grid search
b. *k*-means clustering
c. Linear regression
d. Principal component analysis

5) *k*-nearest neighbors is both a classification and a regression technique. True or False?

SOLUTIONS

1) c. The distance between the boundary line and the nearest data point

2) a, Classification report

3) b, F1 score

4) d, Principal component analysis

5) a, False (*k*-NN is a classification technique only)

13

TREE-BASED METHODS

Tree-based learning algorithms, also known as Cart (Classification and Regression Trees), are a popular technique for predicting numeric and categorical outputs.

Tree-based methods, which include decision trees, bagging, random forests, and boosting, are considered highly effective in the space of supervised learning. This is partly due to their high accuracy and versatility as they can be used to predict both discrete and continuous outcomes.

Decision Trees

Decision trees create a decision structure to interpret patterns by splitting data into groups using variables that best split the data into homogenous or numerically relevant groups based on entropy (a measure of variance in the data among different classes). The primary appeal of decision trees is they can be displayed graphically as a tree-like graph and they're easy to explain to non-experts.

Unlike an actual tree, the decision tree is displayed upside down with the leaves located at the bottom or foot of the free. Each branch represents the outcome of a decision/variable and each leaf node represents a class label, such as "Go to beach" or "Stay in." Decision rules are subsequently marked by the path from the root of the tree to a terminal leaf node.

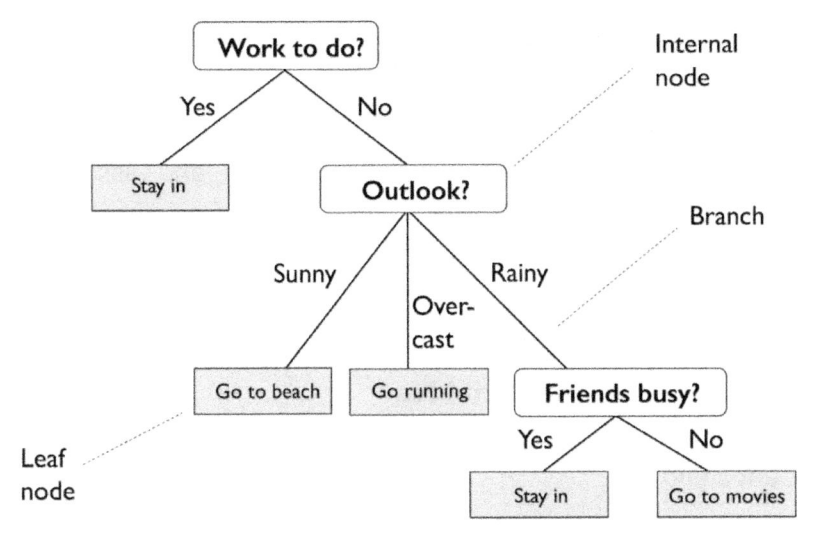

Figure 30: Decision Tree For What To Do Today, Source: https://towardsdatascience.com/

Exercise 1

Let's use a decision tree classifier to predict the outcome of a user clicking on an advert using the Advertising dataset.

1) Import libraries

While decision trees can be used for solving regression or classification problems, this model uses the classification version of the algorithm as we are predicting a discrete variable. Using the `DecisionTreeClassifier` algorithm from Scikit-learn, we will attempt to predict the dependent variable **Clicked on Ad** (0 or 1).[19] The performance of the model will be evaluated using a classification report and a confusion matrix.

```
import pandas as pd
from sklearn.model_selection import train_test_split
from sklearn.tree import DecisionTreeClassifier
```

---

[19] The alternative to **DecisionTreeClassifier** in Scikit-learn is **DecisionTreeRegressor**, and is used for solving regression problems.

```
from sklearn.metrics import classification_report, confusion_matrix
```

2) Import dataset

Import the Advertising Dataset as a dataframe and assign a variable name for the dataset.

```
df = pd.read_csv('~/Downloads/advertising.csv')
```

3) Convert non-numeric variables

Convert the **Country** and **City** variables to numeric values using one-hot encoding.

```
df = pd.get_dummies(df, columns=['Country','City'])
```

4) Remove columns

Remove the discrete variables **Ad Topic Line** and **Timestamp**, which aren't relevant and practical for use with this model.

```
del df['Ad Topic Line']
del df['Timestamp']
```

Let's now inspect the dataframe.

```
df.head()
```

```
1  import pandas as pd
2  from sklearn.model_selection import train_test_split
3  from sklearn.metrics import classification_report, confusion_matrix
4  from sklearn.tree import DecisionTreeClassifier
5
6  df = pd.read_csv('~/Downloads/advertising.csv')
7
8  df = pd.get_dummies(df, columns=['Country','City'])
9
10 del df['Ad Topic Line']
11 del df['Timestamp']
12
13 df.head()
```

	Daily Time Spent on Site	Age	Area Income	Daily Internet Usage	Male	Clicked on Ad	Country_Afghanistan	Country_Albania	Country_Algeria	Country_American Samoa
0	68.95	35	61833.90	256.09	0	0	0	0	0	0
1	80.23	31	68441.85	193.77	1	0	0	0	0	0
2	69.47	26	59785.94	236.50	0	0	0	0	0	0
3	74.15	29	54806.18	245.89	1	0	0	0	0	0
4	68.37	35	73889.99	225.58	0	0	0	0	0	0

5) Set X and y variables

Clicked on Ad serves as the dependent variable (y) for this exercise, while the remaining variables constitute our independent variables (X). The independent variables are **Daily Time Spent on Site**, **Age**, **Area Income**, **Daily Internet Usage**, **Male**, **Country**, and **City**.

```
X = df.drop('Clicked on Ad',axis=1)
y = df['Clicked on Ad']
```

Split the data 70/30, shuffle, and set the random state to 10.

```
X_train, X_test, y_train, y_test = train_test_split(X, y,
test_size=0.3, random_state=10, shuffle=True)
```

6) Set algorithm

Assign `DecisionTreeClassifier()` to the variable **model**.

```
model = DecisionTreeClassifier()
```

Now fit this variable containing the decision tree algorithm to the X and y training data to build our model.

```
model.fit(X_train,y_train)
```

7) Evaluate

Test the training model on the X test data using the `predict` function and assign a new variable name.

```
model_predict = model.predict(X_test)
```

Use a confusion matrix and classification report to review the predictions of the model against the y test data.

```
print(confusion_matrix(y_test, model_predict))
print(classification_report(y_test, model_predict))
```

Run the model.

```
[[136  10]
 [  9 145]]
             precision    recall  f1-score   support

          0       0.94      0.93      0.93       146
          1       0.94      0.94      0.94       154

avg / total       0.94      0.94      0.94       300
```

The model produced 10 false-positives and 9 false-negatives. Let's see if we can improve predictive accuracy using multiple decision trees in the next exercise.

Documentation for Decision Trees: http://bit.ly/2YVVeu4

Random Forests

While decision trees are useful for explaining a model's decision structure, this technique is also prone to overfitting.

In general, decision trees are accurate at decoding patterns using the training data, but because there is a fixed sequence of decision paths, any variance in the test data or new data can result in poor predictions. The fact that there is only one tree design also limits the flexibility of this method to manage variance and future outliers.

A solution for mitigating overfitting is to grow multiple trees using a different technique called random forests. This method involves growing multiple decision trees using a randomized selection of input data for each tree and combining the results by averaging the output for regression or class voting for classification.

The variables selected for dividing the data are also randomized and capped. If the entire forest inspected a full set of variables, each tree would look similar, as the trees would each attempt to maximize information gain at the subsequent layer and thereby select the optimal variable at each split.

Unlike a standard decision tree, though, which has a full set of variables to draw from, the random forests algorithm has an artificially limited set of variables available to build decisions. Due to fewer variables shown and the randomized data provided, random forests are less likely to generate a collection of similar trees. Embracing randomness and volume, random forests are subsequently capable of providing a reliable result with potentially less variance and overfitting than a single decision tree.

Exercise 2

This exercise is a repeat attempt of the previous exercise, again using the Advertising dataset and the same dependent and independent variables but built using `RandomForestClassifier` from Scikit-learn.

1) Import libraries

Note there are two separate algorithms from Scikit-learn for building random forests based on classification or regression. In this exercise, we are utilizing the classification form of the algorithm using Scikit-learn's `RandomForestClassifier` rather than `RandomForestRegressor`, which is used for regression.

```
import pandas as pd
from sklearn.model_selection import train_test_split
from sklearn.ensemble import RandomForestClassifier
from sklearn.metrics import classification_report, confusion_matrix
```

2) Import dataset

Import the advertising dataset.

```
df = pd.read_csv('~/Downloads/advertising.csv')
```

3) Convert non-numeric variables

Use one-hot encoding to convert the variables **Country** and **City** to numeric values.

```
df = pd.get_dummies(df, columns=['Country', 'City'])
```

4) Remove variables

Remove the following two variables from the dataframe.

```
del df['Ad Topic Line']
del df['Timestamp']
```

5) Set X and y variables

Assign the same X and y variables, and split the data 70/30.

```
X = df.drop('Clicked on Ad',axis=1)
y = df['Clicked on Ad']

X_train, X_test, y_train, y_test = train_test_split(X, y,
test_size=0.3, random_state=10, shuffle=True)
```

6) Set algorithm
Assign a variable name to `RandomForestClassifier` and specify the number of estimators. Starting with 100-150 estimators (trees) is generally a good starting point for this algorithm.

```
model = RandomForestClassifier(n_estimators=150)
```

Fit the algorithm to the training data.
```
model.fit(X_train, y_train)
```

7) Evaluate
Using the predict method, let's predict the X test values and assign them as a new variable.

```
model_predict = model.predict(X_test)
```

Using a confusion matrix and classification report, evaluate the predictions of the model using the X test data contained in `model_predict` against the true output (`y_test`).

```
print(confusion_matrix(y_test, model_predict))
print(classification_report(y_test, model_predict))
```
Run the model.

```
[[141   5]
 [  7 147]]
              precision    recall  f1-score   support

           0       0.95      0.97      0.96       146
           1       0.97      0.95      0.96       154

avg / total       0.96      0.96      0.96       300
```

The model has performed well on the test data with a comparatively lower occurrence of false-positives (5) and false-negatives (7), and a higher f1-score of 0.96, which was 0.94 in the case of the decision tree classifier used in the previous exercise.

Documentation for Random Forests: http://bit.ly/2YYzGwI

Gradient Boosting

Like random forests, boosting provides yet another regression/classification technique for aggregating the outcome of multiple decision trees.

Rather than building random independent variants of a decision tree in parallel, gradient boosting is a sequential method that aims to improve the performance of each subsequent tree. This works by evaluating the performance of weak models and then overweighting subsequent models to mitigate the outcome of instances misclassified in earlier rounds. Instances that were classified correctly at the previous round are also replaced with a higher proportion of instances that weren't accurately classified. While this in effect creates another weak model, the modifications derived from the previous model help the new model to key in on the mistakes made by the previous tree.

The adept ability of the algorithm to learn from its mistakes makes gradient boosting one of the most popular algorithms in machine learning today.

Exercise 3

In this third exercise, we will use gradient boosting to predict the outcome of the Advertising dataset in order to compare the results with the two previous algorithms.

Readers of *Machine Learning for Absolute Beginners Second Edition* will be familiar with the regression variant of gradient boosting, but in this exercise we use the classification version of this algorithm, which predicts a discrete variable and comes with slightly different hyperparameters.

1) Import libraries

This model uses the classification form of Gradient Boosting from Scikit-learn's ensemble package.

```
import pandas as pd
from sklearn.model_selection import train_test_split
from sklearn import ensemble
from sklearn.metrics import classification_report, confusion_matrix
```

2) Import dataset

Import the advertising dataset and assign it as a variable.

```
df = pd.read_csv('~/Downloads/advertising.csv')
```

3) Convert non-numeric variables

Use one-hot encoding to convert the variables **Country** and **City** to numeric values.

```
df = pd.get_dummies(df, columns=['Country', 'City'])
```

4) Remove variables

Remove the following two variables from the dataframe.

```
del df['Ad Topic Line']
del df['Timestamp']
```

5) Set X and y variables

Assign the same X and y variables, and split the data 70/30.

```
X = df.drop('Clicked on Ad',axis=1)
y = df['Clicked on Ad']


X_train, X_test, y_train, y_test = train_test_split(X, y,
test_size=0.3, random_state=10, shuffle=True)
```

6) Set algorithm

Assign a variable name to `GradientBoostingClassifier` and specify the number of estimators. A good starting point for this algorithm is 150-250 estimators (trees), with a learning rate of 0.1 and the default loss argument set to `'deviance'`.

```
model = ensemble.GradientBoostingClassifier(
    n_estimators = 250,
    learning_rate = 0.1,
    max_depth = 5,
    min_samples_split = 4,
    min_samples_leaf = 6,
    max_features = 0.6,
    loss = 'deviance'
)
```

Fit the algorithm to the training data.

```
model.fit(X_train, y_train)
```

7) Evaluate

Use the predict method to predict the X test values and assign it as a new variable.

```
model_predict = model.predict(X_test)
```

Using a confusion matrix and classification report, evaluate the model using the X test data contained in `model_predict` against the true output (`y_test`).

```
print(confusion_matrix(y_test, model_predict))
print(classification_report(y_test, model_predict))
```

Run the model.

```
[[142   4]
 [  7 147]]
             precision    recall  f1-score   support

          0       0.95      0.97      0.96       146
          1       0.97      0.95      0.96       154

avg / total       0.96      0.96      0.96       300
```

The model has performed marginally better than random forests with one less prediction error. The f1-score is still 0.96, which is the same as random forests but an improvement on the earlier decision tree classifier (0.94).

Documentation for Gradient Boosting Classifier: http://bit.ly/2ZT7ZCJ

Exercise 4

In this fourth and final exercise, we will use gradient boosting to predict a numeric target output (regression) in the form of the nightly fee for Airbnb accommodation in Berlin, Germany. After devising our initial model, we will then test a sample listing.

1) Import libraries
Import the following libraries.

```
import pandas as pd
from sklearn.model_selection import train_test_split
from sklearn import ensemble
from sklearn.metrics import mean_absolute_error
```

2) Import dataset
For this regression exercise we are using the Berlin Airbnb dataset, which can be downloaded from Kaggle.com.
http://scatterplotpress.com/p/datasets

Feature	Data Type	Continuous/Discrete
id	Integer	Discrete
name	String	Discrete
host_id	Integer	Discrete
host_name	String	Discrete
neighbourhood_group	String	Discrete
neighbourhood	String	Discrete
latitude	String	Discrete
longitude	String	Discrete
room_type	String	Discrete
price	Integer	Continuous
minimum_nights	Integer	Continuous
number_of_reviews	Integer	Continuous
last_review	TimeDate	Discrete
reviews_per_month	Floating-point	Continuous
calculated_host_listings_count	Integer	Continuous
availability_365	Integer	Continuous

Table 18: Berlin Airbnb dataset

Use the `pd.read_csv` command to load the Berlin Airbnb dataset into a Pandas dataframe.

```
# Read in data from CSV
df = pd.read_csv('~/Downloads/listings.csv')
```

3) Remove variables

We won't be using all X variables for our model, partly because there is some information overlap between variables (i.e. **host_name** and **host_id**, as well as **neighborhood** and **neighbourhood_group**). In addition, some variables aren't relevant (i.e. **last_review**), and others are discrete and difficult to parse (i.e. **longitude** and **latitude**).

```
del df['id']
del df['name']
del df['host_name']
del df['last_review']
del df['calculated_host_listings_count']
del df['availability_365']
del df['longitude']
del df['neighbourhood']
del df['latitude']
```

4) Convert non-numeric values

Convert columns that contain non-numeric data to numeric values using one-hot encoding, which in this case is **neighbourhood_group** and **room_type**.

```
df = pd.get_dummies(df, columns = ['neighbourhood_group',
'room_type'])
```

Remove remaining missing values on a row-by-row basis.

```
df.dropna(axis = 0, how = 'any', subset = None, inplace = True)
```

5) Set X and y variables
Assign the X and y variables. The X array contains the independent variables, and the y array contains the dependent variable of price.

```
X = df.drop('price',axis=1)
y = df['price']
```

We are now at the stage of splitting the data into training and test segments. For this exercise, we'll proceed with a standard 70/30 split by calling the Scikit-learn command below with a `test_size` of 0.3 (30%).

```
X_train, X_test, y_train, y_test = train_test_split(X, y,
test_size=0.3, random_state=10, shuffle=True)
```

6) Set algorithm
Assign a variable name to `GradientBoostingRegressor` imported from Scikit-learn's ensemble library, and set the initial hyperparameters as demonstrated below.

```
model = ensemble.GradientBoostingRegressor(
    n_estimators = 350,
    learning_rate = 0.1,
    max_depth = 5,
    min_samples_split = 4,
    min_samples_leaf = 6,
    max_features = 0.6,
    loss = 'huber'
```

)

Use the fit function to assign the algorithm to the training data.

```
model.fit(X_train, y_train)
```

7) Evaluate

Use `mean_absolute_error` from Scikit-learn to compare the difference between the model's expected predictions using `X_train` and the actual values of `y_train`. In this example, the accuracy of the model will display up to two decimal places (`%.2f`).

```
mae_train = mean_absolute_error(y_train, model.predict(X_train))
print ("Training Set Mean Absolute Error: %.2f" % mae_train)
```

The same process is repeated using the test data.

```
mae_test = mean_absolute_error(y_test, model.predict(X_test))
print ("Test Set Mean Absolute Error: %.2f" % mae_test)
```

Run the entire model. The results will appear in your notebook after completion.

```
Training Set Mean Absolute Error: 22.94
Test Set Mean Absolute Error: 22.93
```

After running our model, the training set mean absolute error is $22.94, and the test set mean absolute error is $22.93. This means that on average, the training set miscalculated the actual listing price by $22.94 and the test set by $22.93. The almost identical prediction error between the training and test data indicates low overfitting in our model.

8) Predict

Let's now use our model to predict the overnight price of an individual listing.

```
new_property = [
        2217, #host_id
        4, #minimum_nights
        118, #number_of_reviews
        3.76, #reviews_per_month
        0, #neighbourhood_group_Charlottenburg-Wilm.
        0, #neighbourhood_group_Friedrichshain-Kreuzberg
        0, #neighbourhood_group_Lichtenberg
        0, #neighbourhood_group_Marzahn - Hellersdorf
        1, #neighbourhood_group_Mitte
        0, #neighbourhood_group_Neukölln
        0, #neighbourhood_group_Pankow
        0, #neighbourhood_group_Reinickendorf
        0, #neighbourhood_group_Spandau
        0, #neighbourhood_group_Steglitz - Zehlendorf
        0, #neighbourhood_group_Tempelhof - Schöneberg
        0, #neighbourhood_group_Treptow - Köpenick
        1, #room_type_Entire home/apt
        0, #room_type_Private room
        0, #room_type_Shared room
]

new_pred = model.predict([new_property])
new_pred
```

```
new_property = [
    2217, #host_id
    4, #minimum_nights
    118, #number_of_reviews
    3.76, #reviews_per_month
    0, #neighbourhood_group_Charlottenburg-Wilm.
    0, #neighbourhood_group_Friedrichshain-Kreuzberg
    0, #neighbourhood_group_Lichtenberg
    0, #neighbourhood_group_Marzahn - Hellersdorf
    1, #neighbourhood_group_Mitte
    0, #neighbourhood_group_Neukölln
    0, #neighbourhood_group_Pankow
    0, #neighbourhood_group_Reinickendorf
    0, #neighbourhood_group_Spandau
    0, #neighbourhood_group_Steglitz - Zehlendorf
    0, #neighbourhood_group_Tempelhof - Schöneberg
    0, #neighbourhood_group_Treptow - Köpenick
    1, #room_type_Entire home/apt
    0, #room_type_Private room
    0, #room_type_Shared room
]

new_pred = model.predict([new_property])
new_pred
```

array([67.78851254])

The model predicts that an entire home/apartment located in the neighborhood of Mitte is priced at approximately $67.79 per night. The actual price for this listing is $60 per night and was taken from the first row of the Berlin Airbnb dataset.[20]

Lastly, please take into account that because the training and test data are shuffled randomly, and data is fed to decision trees at random, the predicted results will differ slightly when replicating this model on your own machine.

Documentation for Gradient Boosting Regressor: http://bit.ly/2YGoohl

---

[20] This sample data point may have been included as part of the model's training data, which perhaps explains the low error.

QUIZ

1) Which tree-based technique can be easily visualized?

a. Decision trees
b. Gradient boosting
c. Random forests
d. Bagging

2) Which tree-based technique is prone to overfitting?

a. Decision trees
b. Gradient boosting
c. Random forests
d. Bagging

3) Gradient boosting is an example of a sequential processing algorithm. True or False?

4) Which is not an accurate description of random forests?

a. Ensemble technique
b. Parallel processing algorithm
c. Visualization algorithm
d. Classification technique

5) What is generally a good number of initial estimators (trees) for a gradient boosting classifier?

a. 100
b. 1000
c. 2
d. 150-250

SOLUTIONS

1) a, Decision trees

2) a, Decision trees

3) True

4) c, Visualization algorithm

5) d, 150-250

NEXT STEPS

Having reached the end of this book you are well on your way to coding machine learning models in Python.

Now is also an opportune moment to consider future specializations in machine learning, including recommender systems, natural language processing, fraud detection, and image recognition using artificial neural networks. To learn more about recommender systems, the third book in this series **Machine Learning: Make Your Own Recommender System** provides a beginner's introduction to coding recommender systems using collaborative and content-based filtering.

You can also follow and find free learning materials and videos on my Instagram channel at **machinelearning_beginners** and sign up for my **Newsletter**: **http://eepurl.com/gKjQij**

If you have any direct feedback about aspects of the book you strongly liked or dislike, please feel free to write to me at oliver.theobald@scatterplotpress.com. This feedback is highly valued and I look forward to hearing from you.

Oliver Theobald
August 2019

APPENDIX 1: INTRO TO PYTHON

Python was designed by Guido van Rossum at the National Research Institute for Mathematics and Computer Science in the Netherlands during the late 1980s and early 1990s. Derived from the Unix shell command-line interpreter and other programming languages including C and C++, it was designed to empower developers to write programs with fewer lines of code than other languages.[21] Unlike other programming languages, Python also incorporates many English keywords where other languages use punctuation symbols.

In Python, the input code is read by the Python interpreter to perform an output. Any errors, including poor formatting, misspelled functions, or random characters left someplace in your script are picked up by the Python interpreter and cause a syntax error.

In this chapter we will discuss the basic syntax to help you write fluid and effective code.

Comments

Adding comments is good practice in computer programming to signpost the purpose and content of your code. In Python, comments can be added to your code using the # (hash) symbol. Everything placed after the hash symbol (on that line of code) is then ignored by the Python interpreter.

```
# Import Melbourne Housing dataset from my Downloads folder
dataframe = pd.read_csv('~/Downloads/Melbourne_housing_FULL.csv')
```

---

[21] Mike McGrath, "Python in easy steps: Covers Python 3.7," *In Easy Steps Limited*, Second Edition, 2018.

In this example, the second line of code will be executed, while the first line of code will be ignored by the Python interpreter.

Indentation & Spaces

Unlike other programming languages, Python uses *indentation* to group code statements, such as functions and loops, rather than keywords or punctuation to separate code blocks.

```
new_user = [
    66.00, #Daily Time Spent on Site
    48, #Age
    24593.33, #Area Income
    131.76, #Daily Internet Usage
    1, #Male
    0, #Country_Afghanistan
    1, #Country_ Albania
    0, #Country_Algeria
]
```

Spaces, though, in expressions are ignored by the Python interpreter, i.e. 8+4 or 8 + 4, but can be added for (human) clarity.

Python Data Types

Common data types in Python are shown in the following table.

Name	Explanation	Key Feature	Example
Integer	Whole numbers	No decimal point	50
Floating-point	Numbers with a decimal placing	Decimal point	50.1
String	Words and characters	Single/double quote marks	"Fifty5" or 'Fifty5'
List	Ordered sequence of objects	Square brackets	[1, 2, 3, 4, 'fifty']
Tuple	An order and immutable sequence of objects. Almost the same as a list, except values cannot be manipulated, thereby guaranteeing data integrity by preventing accidental changes in complex pieces of code.	Parenthesis	(1, 2, 3, 4)
Dictionary	Key-value pair. The key is denoted by a string such as a file name and linked to a value such as an image or text.	Curly brackets, colon, and quote marks	{"name" : "john", "gender" : "male"}
Set	An unordered collection of unique objects	Curly brackets	{"1", "2", "a"}
Booleans	Binary values	Capital initial (T/F)	**True** or **False**

Table 19: Common Python data types

In machine learning, you'll most commonly be working with lists containing strings, integers, or floating-point numbers. String variables are also called *character* or *alphanumeric variables* and can include alphabetic letters, numbers, and symbols such as a hashtag (#) or underscore (_).

Arithmetic in Python

Commonly used arithmetical operators in Python are displayed in Table 20.

Operator	Explanation	Sample Input	Output
+	Addition	2 + 2	4
-	Subtraction	2 - 2	0
*	Multiplication	2 * 2	4
/	Division	5 / 2	2.5
%	Mod function (the remainder after division)	5 % 2	1
//	Floor division (removes the remainder after decimal point)	5 // 2	2
**	Exponent	2 ** 3	8

Table 20: Commonly used arithmetical operators in Python

Python adheres to the standard mathematical order of operations, such that multiplication or division, for example, is executed before addition or subtraction.

```
2 + 2 * 3
```
The output of this equation is 8.

As with standard arithmetic, parentheses can be added to modify the sequence of operations, as shown below.

```
(2 + 2) * 3
```
The output of this equation is 12.

Variable Assignment

In computer programming, the role of a variable is to store a data value in the computer's memory for later use. This enables earlier code to be referenced and manipulated by the Python interpreter calling that variable name. You can select any name for the variable granted it fits with the following rules:
- It contains only alpha-numeric characters and underscores (A-Z, 0-9, _)
- It starts with a letter or underscore and not a number
- It does not imitate a Python keyword such as "print" or "return"

In addition, variable names are case-sensitive, such that `dataframe` and `Dataframe` are considered two separate variables. Variables are assigned in Python using the = operator.

```
dataset = 8
```

Python, though, does not support blank spaces between variable keywords and an underscore must be used to link variable keywords.

```
my_dataset = 8
```

The stored value (8) can now be referenced by calling the variable name `my_dataset`.

Variables also have a "variable" nature, in that we can reassign the variable to a different value, such as:

```
my_dataset = 8 + 8
```

The value of the `my_dataset` is now 16.

It's important to note that the equals operator in Python does not serve the same function as equals in mathematics. In Python, the equals operator assigns variables but does not follow mathematical logic. If you wish to solve a mathematical equation in Python you can simply run the code without adding an equals operator.

```
2 + 2
```

Python will return 4 in this case.

If you want to confirm whether a mathematical relationship in Python is True or False, you can use ==.

```
2 + 2 == 4
```

Python will return `True` in this case.

The Print Function

The `print()` function is used to print a message within its parentheses and is one of the most used functions in Python. Given its uncomplicated utility—returning exactly what you want printed—it might not seem an important programming function or even necessary. But this is not true.

Firstly, print is useful for debugging (finding and fixing code errors). After adjusting a variable, for example, you can check the current value using the print function.

```
my_dataset = 8
my_dataset = 8 + 8
print(my_dataset)
```

Output: `16`

Another common use case is to print non-processible information as a string. This means that the statement/string enclosed in the parentheses is directly printed and doesn't interact with other elements of the code. This feature is useful for adding context and clarity to your code by annotating aspects of the code—especially as code comments (#) don't show as an output.

Input: `print ("Training Set Mean Absolute Error: %.2f" % mae_train)`

Output: `Training Set Mean Absolute Error: 27834.12`

This print statement, for example, informs the end-user of what was processed by the Python interpreter to deliver that result. Without **print("Test Set Mean Absolute Error:")**, all we'd see is unlabeled numbers after the code has been executed.

Please note the string inside the parentheses must be wrapped with double-quote marks " " or single quote marks ' '. A mixture of single and double-quote marks is invalid. The print function automatically removes the quote marks after you run the code. If you wish to include quote marks in the output, you can add single quote marks inside double-quote marks as shown here:

Input: `print("'Test Set Mean Absolute Error'")`
Output: `'Test Set Mean Absolute Error'`

Input: `print("What's your name?")`
Output: `What's your name?`

Indexing

Indexing is a method of selecting a single element from inside a data type, such as a list or string. Each element in a data type is numerically indexed beginning at 0, and elements can be indexed by calling the index number inside square brackets.

Example 1
`my_string = "hello_world"`
`my_string[1]`

Indexing returns the value **e** in this example.

Element:	h	e	l	l	o	_	w	o	r	l	d
Index:	0	1	2	3	4	5	6	7	8	9	10

Example 2
`my_list = [10, 20 , 30 , 40]`
`my_list[0]`

Indexing returns the value **10** in this example.

Element:	10	20	30	40
Index:	0	1	2	3

Slicing

Rather than pull a single element from a collection of data, you can use slicing to grab a customized subsection of elements using a colon (:).

Example 1

`my_list = [10, 20, 30, 40]`

`my_list[:3]`

Slicing, here, goes up to but does not include the element at index position 3, thereby returning the values **10**, **20**, and **30**.

Example 2

`my_list = [10, 20, 30, 40]`

`my_list[1:3]`

Slicing, here, starts at 1 and goes up to but does not include the element at index position 3, thereby returning the values **20** and **30** in this example.

APPENDIX 2: PRINT COLUMNS

A code shortcut for printing columns with the necessary formatting to use as input for model prediction, as discussed in Chapter 10, can be generated using the following code.

```
cols = df.columns.tolist()
print("new_project = [")
for item in cols:
    print("\t0, "+"#"+item)
print("]")
```

Run the temporary code in Jupyter Notebook.

```
cols = df.columns.tolist()
print("new_project = [")
for item in cols:
    print("\t0, "+"#"+item)
print("]")

new_project = [
        0, #Comments
        0, #Rewards
        0, #Goal
        0, #Backers
        0, #Duration in Days
        0, #Facebook Friends
        0, #Facebook Shares
        0, #Creator - # Projects Created
        0, #Creator - # Projects Backed
        0, ## Videos
        0, ## Images
        0, ## Words (Description)
        0, ## Words (Risks and Challenges)
        0, ## FAQs
        0, #State_successful
        0, #Currency_CAD
        0, #Currency_EUR
        0, #Currency_GBP
        0, #Currency_NZD
        0, #Currency_USD
```

Now copy and paste the code output you have generated back into the notebook for the next section of your code. Also note that this temporary code prints all variables (including X and y variables) and you may need to remove the dependent variable (y) from the code, which in this case is `state_successful`.

OTHER BOOKS BY THE AUTHOR

Available on Amazon

AI for Absolute Beginners

Published in 2023, this book is the complete guide for beginners to AI, including easy-to-follow breakdowns of natural language processing, generative AI, deep learning, recommender systems, and computer vision.

Generative AI Art for Beginners

Master the use of text prompts to generate stunning AI art in seconds.

ChatGPT Prompts Book

Maximize your results with ChatGPT using a series of proven text prompt strategies.

Machine Learning for Absolute Beginners

Learn the fundamentals of machine learning, explained in plain English.

Machine Learning: Make Your Own Recommender System

Learn how to make your own machine learning recommender system in an afternoon using Python.

Data Analytics for Absolute Beginners

Make better decisions using every variable with this deconstructed introduction to data analytics.

Statistics for Absolute Beginners

Master the fundamentals of inferential and descriptive statistics with a mix of practical demonstrations, visual examples, historical origins, and plain English explanations.

Python for Absolute Beginners

Master the essentials of Python from scratch with beginner-friendly guidance.

Printed in Great Britain
by Amazon